"As a writer and collector of st
sent dozens of stories and arti
information very good but in the end confusing. I have to say
that Marilyn Gordon's perspective is as high as it gets and it
clears the mind and heart. What she writes about is truth. I
appreciate her wisdom and clarity in conveying her ideas."

> – Darlene Montgomery, Author, Conscious
> Women, Conscious Lives. Lifedreams
> Communications

"The golden wisdom and skills I learned from Marilyn have
healed me and opened up my path for my soul completion. I
want to take this opportunity to express my gratitude. I am
practicing all that I have learned from her, especially the
Wise Mind Process. The wisdom she has passed on to me
has changed and healed my life giving me the chance to help
my family and others. My heart is full with gratitude."

> – Deniz Keller, Hypnotherapist

"The Wise Mind is a really great book. After reading it, I
feel so empowered. I feel in charge of my life, able to decide
where I go, what to eat, and how I feel. It's a wonderful
thing. Thank you so very much for this. Reading this has
transformed me."

> – Phyllis Hoosin, Retired

"Marilyn is my main catalyst for bringing my life work out into the world."

– Gayle Greco, Hypnotherapist and
Teacher

"Toss your collection of self-help books! In our modern American culture we have lost the tradition of the Wise Woman. Marilyn Gordon is such a person. She opens us up to our Wise Mind and the Wise Mind Process for true healing and transformation. And as we connect to the Ultimate Reality, we can finally let go of our stories of lack and limitation and return to expanded awareness where we find true healing, deep peace and the ultimate truth of love, wisdom, light, forgiveness, and enlightenment."

– Gina Orlando, Hypnotherapist

"Marilyn Gordon is a Master Teacher here on Earth. I saw that truth the first time our eyes met. It is heartwarming to be sharing this planet with one such as her. She is part of the grand plan of orchestrating a change based in the enlightenment and upliftment of humanity. She has had a part to play in the awareness of the impact of empathy and compassion, and she works for the betterment of humanity."

Kathleen Schramm, Intuitive and Radio Host

The Wise Mind

The Brilliant Key
to Life Transformation
and Healing

Marilyn Gordon

WiseWord Publishing
Oakland CA

WiseWord Publishing
PO Box 10795
Oakland CA 94610

Printed in the Untied States of America
Book Design by Carla Radosta
Cover Graphics by Amy and Nancy Rector of
Cyclops Studios

ISBN 1440469741

Dedication

This book is dedicated to the infinite
forces of love and wisdom,
as they manifest in us and serve
as the primary agents for
transformation and healing

The Wise Mind is the higher faculty
of advanced consciousness, wisdom, or guidance
that is innate in every human being.
It's the part of the Self that can stand back
and see from a greater perspective.
Brilliant wisdom is within every being.
It's brilliant because we are a reflection
of the great Universe itself.
The Wise Mind is part and parcel of the
Universal Source, as it exists in
microcosmic form within us.

- Marilyn Gordon -

With Gratitude

Dianne Kathryn Short, who has worked with me for almost twenty years, and who is my eagle eyes and my dear compassionate friend; Victoria King, high-energy being who gets so many things done while remaining always in a state of love and joy; Linda Anson, a loving person who knows how to be of service and who has a true knack for sending products all over the world; John Anson, an invaluable human being, the master of high tech and the overseer of our computers; Priscilla Stuckey for her great editorial contributions; Amy and Nancy Rector of Cyclops Studios for their brilliant artwork; Gina Chiotti-Hovey, who lovingly takes care of our numbers and spreadsheets; Carla Radosta, who has a genius for design and who designed this book and Julie Cline for production/layout; excellent teachers in our wonderful school: Dianne Kathryn Short, Hollis Polk, Seth-Deborah Roth, Gerri Levitas, and Beverly Taylor, and our excellent workshop instructors; students and clients—we love you; Brian Choate, who is an amazing technical wizard; Sarah Horton for her creative wisdom; Arnold Patent and Wendie Webber for editorial assistance; Teri Williams for creative photography; David Klein, of Living Nutrition, for miraculous healing inspiration; Aunt Phyllis, who is and always has been loving and kind; Nada Gordon, my daughter, a magnificent writer who lives in creative inspiration; family on the Other Side with appreciation for their great assistance; the Sages and Masters, whose wisdom has graced my life for so many years and now these pages; the Universal Power of Love and Wisdom, God, who illumines my life.

Contents

Part Two 93
What Your Wise Mind Might Tell You

Wise Mind Questions and Answer

What's the difference between the Wise Mind and the conscious or subconscious mind?

What if I have a hard time describing my situation? What am I supposed to be looking for?

What if I can't see my situation breaking up into tiny molecules?

What if emotions come up?

How do I know it's really the Wise Mind speaking? How do I know what it's telling me is true?

When I go deeply inside, I'm afraid I'll find something negative or hard to deal with. What should I do?

What if my Wise Mind tells me the wise things to do, but another part of me doesn't want to listen?

What if I need to do a lot of deep inner healing?

Can this help with physical issues and health situations, like illness, pain, or headaches?

Can I do this work with someone else—with a family member or mate? What if he or she won't do it?

How can I do this work with a group?

How can I do this work as a healing practitioner?

What if I need to tell someone how I feel, to communicate my grievances? What if I need to work out an issue with someone and not just myself?

What if it doesn't work for me?

I want to heal and transform, but I have so many obstacles. I feel that something is in my way. What can I do?

What if similar situations keep coming up in my life?

I know I'm a healer, but I've had such a difficult life, and I'm not perfect. Can I still help others?

What if I do the Wise Mind Process and more and more issues come up?

Do I need to find the root cause of my issue in order to heal and transform it?

Is it really possible to heal?

Introduction

This is a book about the Wise Mind. That is obvious – but what may not be obvious is how crucial the Wise Mind is in healing the problems of life. For years I've asked many people seeking inner healing to open up new ways of understanding their challenges. What happens always when we've done this is that we're moved into alternate levels of consciousness where solutions present themselves often in extraordinary ways. This book is about leaping into advanced levels of mind in which the powers of healing and transformation come alive.

Underneath the experience of wounds, pain, and grief there is an even more powerful reality of wisdom and love. At the core of being there is also light, peace, compassion, and bliss. These are the magnificent gifts we're given for healing, and there are powerful ways to open them. That's what *The Wise Mind* is all about.

Thank you for opening these pages and for advancing your journey of self knowledge, wisdom, and inner light.

With love and blessings to you,
Marilyn Gordon

"The Wise Mind, also called

the superconscious state, is a natural part

of the self, as natural as love,

and when we come into contact with it,

we are given a tool that shifts the

very core of our life.

It's the crown jewel of

states of consciousness, and it is

the remedy for all the issues

and difficulties of life."

Part One

Brilliant Transformational Power

Chapter One

The Fascinating Truth about the Wise Mind

It's in every one of us
To be wise.
Find your heart, open up both your eyes.
We could all know everything without ever knowing why.
It's in every one of us by and by.
—David Pomeranz, *"It's in Every One of Us"*

You are a being of true magnificence and power, and you can resolve and transform the challenges of your life through the brilliance of your own Wise Mind. You can move from the illusion of darkness to the reality of light, from your limited self to your essence. Through your Wise Mind and the amazing process of transformation, you can set yourself free.

In this book you'll learn how to access your Wise Mind and its revelations. You'll learn the Wise Mind Process, an original and astoundingly simple yet powerful way to resolve your challenges moment by moment. The process is filled with enlightenment and power. You'll learn ways to transform your life so that you can operate on the highest levels.

Through this altered perception, you can handle fears and negative thoughts, relationships, sadness, anger, stress, losses, self-deprecation—everything that you perceive to limit you—-and you can experience huge shifts in well-being, health, work, relationships, and spiritual growth. You'll learn specific ways to release obstacles so that you can experience love, wisdom, compassion, and peace and find new knowledge and spiritual wisdom.

You Don't Have to Spend Years Working Things Out

Everyone in one way or another is looking for a way to overcome the challenges of being human. Almost everyone subscribes to realities of limitation, be it pain in your body, economic or relationship challenges, or old traumas or abuses. Whatever you may perceive, everything in your life presents an opportunity. All of it contains the seeds of dynamic transformation. It means that you don't have to spend years working things out. Through the power of your Wise Mind, you can make dynamic shifts to lift yourself into new ways of being. You can step into advanced levels of your life.

You as universal consciousness have creative power. When you step into an expanded understanding, you may see that there is a reality far more potent than your old perceptions of your life. This potent reality is the expanded recognition of your magnificence, love, and power. From this vantage point, what you tell yourself about "what happened to you" is not necessarily the highest truth.

The Wise Mind Presents Itself

The Wise Mind has brilliant transformational power. If you ask the question, "What would my Wise Mind tell me about this?" you can open the door to great revelations and shifts in every part of life.

I regularly ask people, "What would your Wise Mind tell you about that?" Their answers are often fascinating. People from all walks of life and of all ages bring forth wisdom about their life situations that help them to shift their habits, succeed in their careers, remove old blockages, transform their relationships, and dissolve their anger and fear.

What Exactly Is the Wise Mind?

In essence, the Wise Mind is the eternal wisdom of your soul, a part of the infinite wisdom of the Universe. It is the part of you that knows. My eighty-four year old Aunt Phyllis said to me, "I know what the Wise Mind is. My Wise Mind is God sending me my right thoughts."

We travel far and wide to find answers. We visit shamans and shrines, teachers and sages, and yet we have in the inner terrain of consciousness a vast network of truth, a universal system that exists as a microcosm within us ready to let us know what is the greatest path to follow, the wisest ways to look at our lives, and the most effective ways to transform ourselves. Not that there is anything wrong with visiting outer sources. This is often important and necessary. Yet there is a place of truth and knowing in the inner depths of being that we can't deny.

The Wise Mind is brilliant, but not in the same way as the intellect. The Wise Mind is brilliant because its wisdom transcends ordinary awareness and shines like a million stars. It is all-knowing divine energy, alive in us since the beginning of time.

The Wise Mind, also called the superconscious state, is a natural part of the self, as natural as love, and when we come into contact with it, we are given a tool that shifts the very core of our life. It's the crown jewel of states of consciousness, and it is the remedy for all the issues and difficulties of life. The Wise Mind, along with its brothers and sisters, love, peace, light, forgiveness, bliss, healing, and enlightenment, are all forms of divine experience. When we work with the Wise Mind, we tap in to the vast pool of the superconscious system of the Universe, our innate resource for becoming enlightened and transformed.

A Major Shift for Denise

Denise had broken her foot, and after three months she was still on crutches. She wondered why it was taking so long. At one point she even began to cry, as she said, "I miss my body. I miss running and doing yoga, going barefoot, walking down the hall." Her Wise Mind spoke to her and said:

> Everything's okay. Everything is as it should be. There is no problem. Don't worry. Be gentle with yourself. All things, objects, people are in the exact proper order. There is nothing out of place here, and you were sent no curve ball. This is part of your expansion. You will walk again with great ease—and a little lighter as well. Move with stillness.

Denise imagined herself standing, doing yoga with a new lightness about her, understanding that her broken foot was a blessing and a teacher. She now had a different way of expressing her energy, a movement in stillness.

She then had an image of a pond with lotus blossoms. The wind made very calm ripples across the pond. She was sitting on the edge of the shore of this garden pond, surrounded by willow trees and pastel flowers, perched on a rock looking at the pond and the pink lotuses. The sun was filtering through and reflecting off the pond. There was peace, enormous peace. Her Wise Mind spoke again:

> This is who you really are. At the bottom of everything, this is who you are. You're enveloped in this warmth and beauty, the sky is blue, and the flowers are gently pink. Seeing this, your foot is healed. You remember the message: "Move with stillness.'"

Change Is Different from Transformation

Like Denise, you can learn through your Wise Mind not to change, but to transform. Many books have been written about how to change your life. But change is something different from transformation. Change is something done over time, piece by piece. It assumes that something is not perfect, though everything in your world has its own perfection. Transformation, however, is a dynamic alteration of the perspectives from which you live. It's about transforming your ways of seeing life on an ongoing basis. Through your Wise Mind, you experience life from an altered dimension. You move to a greater reality, into another level of being, and from this expanded space, your issues transform. Transformation is seeing the perfection at the heart of all that is.

My Path to the Wise Mind

I began to understand the miraculous transformational qualities of the Wise Mind in the seventies when I learned yoga and meditation. In my old perceived reality, I needed both desperately, having been a high school English teacher in a school that had succumbed to the riots of the late sixties. I needed to relax, to find a place to rest my head. I perceived great turmoil in my life—with relationship, family, and my work. When yoga and meditation showed me a new way of being and I learned how to become the witness of my mind and tap in to my higher consciousness states, I changed every part of my life—from my work to my way of eating and living. Whenever I felt the call, I tuned my dial to the brilliant Wise Mind and asked how I might understand the truth of any situation in my life. I always received answers— some brief, some more lengthy—and I was eternally grateful that I had found a way to step out of the perceived quicksand of old patterns and thoughts and move into another level of self. You'll read about some of these deeper experiences in this book. These early days of discovering the vast resources of the higher mind were revelations to me through what I perceived as challenges of all kinds. My Wise Mind guided me to transform my understanding of them. My Wise Mind spoke to me either in brief phrases or at length in paragraphs or pages, and it became the catalyst for me to shift the very ground of my being. Sometimes I'd just listen; other times I'd get a microphone and recorder or just a pen and paper (and now a computer), and my Wise Mind would give me an alternative view of my challenges. This way, it always transformed me.

I learned to look at the images inside my mind and consciousness as well, and I created a form of inner healing that helped people to shift from their deepest troubles to their highest selves. I began to work with people on every issue of human difficulty, assisting them to alter their perception. I developed the Wise Mind Process, which you'll read about here. It's a process that can help you transform every issue of your life.

The material in the Wise Mind Process and in the rest of this book is based on yoga philosophy, Eastern psychology, metaphysics, and modern inner technologies of transformation. The stories you'll read come from thousands of hours of assisting people with their processes of transformation—listening to them and guiding them to move from darkness into light.

This book is for you and for your path with the deepest wishes that your own Wise Mind will guide you on the great path of transformation and healing.

What You'll Find in This Book

Keep reading to find much more about the Wise Mind and how it can help you to make breakthroughs in your life. Here are some of the places we'll go as you read on:

- Recognize the various qualities of the Wise Mind

- Make contact with your Wise Mind

- Find out what your Wise Mind might tell you, powerful truths that will guide you to release your issues and transform your consciousness and your life

- Learn the powerful Wise Mind Process and how it can help you to transform the challenges of your life simply and deeply, as well as inspire you to move into states of greater happiness, creativity, and peace

- Read many stories of transformation through the Wise Mind and the Wise Mind Process

- Learn how to create your own inner Wise Mind workshop

- Use meditations and scripts to illuminate your life

Seek the Great Inner Force

When you experience yourself as separate from the essence of all life, you may have feelings and experiences that reinforce this separation. When you're in tune, you may experience love, light, and wisdom. Transformation is about renewing the connection with your source. When you ask the Wise Mind to assist you to mend the rift, you come back to wisdom, love, and peace.

The lyrical and mystical poet Rumi consistently invited us to look inside:

> There is a force within that gives you life—
> Seek that.
> In your body there lies a priceless jewel—
> Seek that.
> If you are in search of the greatest treasure,
> don't look outside.
> Look within, and seek That.[i]

As you read on, I hope you will find a place to rest your head and your heart also. I hope the Wise Mind Process will help you to shine the light on anything that is ready for transformation in your life. You can always look to the Wise Mind and the eternal wisdom of your soul.

Chapter Two

Getting to Know Your Wise Mind

When you have found your true soul-nature of everlasting joy,
that indestructible bliss will remain with you though all experiences of life.

—Paramahansa Yogananda, Man's Eternal Quest

If each of us holds within us a reflection of the Great Wisdom, where does the Wise Mind reside? And how do we find its wisdom? Once we've learned how to contact our Wise Mind, how can we consistently recognize its voice? These are questions we'll answer as we get to know The Wise Mind.

Where Does the Wise Mind Reside?

Your mind includes several levels of consciousness, and the Wise Mind is an integral part of one of them. The first of these levels, the conscious mind, is your thinking mind. Its job is to judge, be logical, evaluate, and take in the facts of the world through its own interpretations. Too often it gets mired in these interpretations, such as when it appears that a rope you see is a snake or when you think that everything must be judged. This is not the realm of the Wise Mind. It's the conscious mind, and we live here a great deal of the time. When you stand back and look at your conscious mind, you may come to understand that what you're seeing is your own creation, your own interpretation of what only seems to be real.

The next level is not the realm of the Wise Mind either. It's the subconscious mind, the data storage or filing Isystem of consciousness. Everything that you perceive has happened to you is stored here and cataloged. This includes losses, pain, habits, and traumas, and it also includes subpersonalities like the inner child. You can put it on "search mode" and find out the possible antecedents to current issues. You don't have to dwell in this area to learn about yourself and your creations, and yet it holds its own fascination as the great search engine of the inner being. Nevertheless, when you look at it from an expanded point of view, you may come to understand that what you've saved in your subconscious mind are actually semblances of what is truly real, collections of beliefs and perceptions that are not seeing into the true nature of things.

The unconscious mind stores records of all your patterns that you've brought to this lifetime, such as tendencies to feel "I'll never be any good" or "I'm better than everyone." These, of course, are illusions too.

The energy field is your aura or electromagnetic field. Tapping the code of your energy field can create healing and relief from difficulties and discomforts.

Now for the place where the Wise Mind takes up residence. It is a part of the supreme state of consciousness, the superconscious state, the transformation system of the universe. The qualities of this state—wisdom, love, peace, light, forgiveness, and enlightenment—are gifts given to us. The superconscious state goes above and beyond every other feeling, thought, pattern, or tendency in our body and mind, and our awareness of it shifts the very core of our life itself.

The conscious mind and the subconscious mind are the repositories of the dilemmas or illusions, and the Wise Mind is the representative and voice of the soul, an inborn remedy of transformation.

The Revolution in Consciousness

We're shifting out of our old ways of working with our difficulties. Something big is happening in the area of inner transformation, and it's big enough so it's the force that can ultimately transform our world. We're shifting from our traditional paradigms to a transformational mind-set. This is a big shift, a leap from "improving yourself" into experiencing the eternal essence of yourself. In this inner part of yourself, there is already everything you need and want. Here all solutions lie, and this revolution in consciousness is taking you to a profound next step.

Transformation, the "New" Paradigm

Transformation, again, is a process of moving from the illusion of darkness into the reality of light. It can shift you out of your troubles into states of great understanding. Because we see the events of our lives through the filters of our own experiences, we see them "through a glass darkly." We don't see things as they really are. There are, however, illumined ways of seeing that powerfully shift the way we understand all the old events of our lives. And even though this is timeless knowledge, it's actually revolutionary. Every moment, we get to experience this knowledge in a whole new way.

Moses and His Wife

You no doubt remember the blockbuster movie, "The Ten Commandments." In one scene, the movie-Moses is talking to his wife. His wife is beside herself, bemoaning the fate of their people, who've been suffering for so many years. Moses says to her, "Yes, but that is because you're not seeing the entire picture." Moses was telling her that there is a huge transformation taking place in social, political, and spiritual history, and, being human, she can't see what's happening in its fullest perspective. That's almost always the case with every one of us, that every one of our travails, large and small, is an opportunity to move into an expanded state of learning, growth, and understanding.

Enlightened Understanding

Here in this book you'll find a way to do this for yourself. This process of transformation can lead you from confusion to clarity, from turmoil to peace. Transforming your consciousness is a way of paying attention to what's taking place within you—and then moving your awareness to higher ground. You'll be able make contact with the Wise Mind, and you'll also see how to experience and then release the issues of your life so that you can lift yourself up into higher states of awareness. We'll also look at transformed ways of looking at your life and other approaches to reaching higher states of consciousness. Yet there's more to this process than communicating with the Wise Mind. This is a process that involves a few steps to make the healing more complete. It's appropriately called the "Wise Mind Process," and you'll find out all about it in the following chapters

Chapter Three

Remember the Truth of Who You Are

*The truth is that there is nothing outside of us;
all that we see is our Self. This becomes our
new reality when we open the belief in separation
and accept the truth that we are the Power of God.*

—Arnold Patent, The Journey

The Wise Mind Presents Alternatives

The greatest alternative to ordinary awareness is that is that you can leap into an entirely different paradigm or state of consciousness—the consciousness of the Wise Mind—and the transformation will take place without your needing to find any apparent causation for the problem at all. Actually, the truth is that not being connected with the expanded view in the first place is the real cause of the problem. The truth is that the separation from our true nature, which you can call the separation from God, the Universe, the Oneness, is the real cause of limitations and difficulties.

The "cure" then is to reconnect ourselves with this expanded state of awareness. That's why many affirmative statements, especially those that begin with "I AM," can bring us back to the place of wholeness. These are actually beyond affirmations. They are statements of the truth. These may sound like: "I AM the light of the universe" or "I AM the power of healing now and always" or "I AM the Power and Presence of God." It's this awareness of the expanded self that ultimately unites us once again with the true power of transformation.

What Are The Alternatives?

Most of the great texts, sutras, and mystical teachings (including *A Course in Miracles*) say that there is an underlying and overriding reality that you can call the Self or the Essence or the All That Is. So when we get caught up in the illusion, then the problems and challenges come. When we return to the expanded truth of the Essence, then we come back to the real understanding of what is taking place. Ordinarily, we don't see things the way they really are, and so we get mired in suffering. We can stay there and do what we can to "cure" it within that framework, but the real next step is to leap out of the paradigm and move into states of consciousness in which the suffering is transformed.

The Wise Mind Creates Perspective

As you'll see in chapter 5, there is a powerful process that can assist you in moving from the illusion of darkness into the reality of light. First you allow yourself time and space to experience your difficulty. You look at it and describe it, and then you release it. Then through the Wise Mind, you bring yourself to a view of the possibilities of a transformed existence. The Wise Mind takes you to new states of consciousness, to love, peace, light, and wisdom, and these shift your very ground of being.

Still, as I mentioned, it's often interesting to play in the arena of the apparent cause of the situation, to think that because you may have had a significant trauma, for example, that the trauma itself is a cause of your apparent dysfunction. It may be an antecedent, and it may appear to have a profound connection to the issue at hand—but there's a bigger truth: that you're looking at things through the lens of a smaller paradigm and that making a leap into a larger one is the solution.

This larger paradigm is that there is a deep and high reality that supersedes and infuses all of matter and form. This is the Field, the Force, the Eternal Energy, God, and All That Is. Many of the greatest sages tell us that the reason we came to this Earth is to once again remember this Force. As we live life, we present apparent challenges to ourselves, and if we get the messages in them, they can be catalysts for us to move into greater enlightenment. We're here to remember who we are and what our true nature really is. So if you believe that you're ugly or misshapen or poor or downtrodden, you aren't seeing the truth and you're reinforcing it with the power of intent, which is a power of your feelings and mind. The moment you make the shift and remember that you're a part of a great reality, that you're beautiful because you're made of the Essence, that you're a part of Infinite Abundance, that you have a profound power inside, then you've made the leap into a timeless reality.

This is why spiritual or transformational healing is important—because its purpose is to return you time after time to the truth, to undo the illusions of life, and to return you once again to the reality of wholeness and oneness. This is why your leap into the Wise Mind is a giant step into the ultimate transformation.

The Subconscious and The Superconscious

The subconscious mind is a library or a catalog of limited reality, and it in itself cannot get you to the truth. That's why we fortunately have within us the Superconscious mind, the Supreme Consciousness, of which the Wise Mind is a part. It is made of love, light, wisdom, and peace. It is the true cure for what ails us. Getting in touch with it returns us to wholeness and is the basis of prayer, meditation, transformational understanding, and ultimate healing. It is ultimately practical, as it consistently reminds us of the wholeness that is at the core of our being and that we can consistently return to for comfort and peace.

Yogis and sages have said:

> I AM not my body,
> Not my mind.
> Immortal Self I AM.

This means I'm not wretched or poor or dysfunctional or ugly. In truth, I AM something more, and when I understand this, I can move myself out of anxiety and fear, doubt, seeming failure, and limitation. I can remember that I'm a radiant being of the universe, graced with an innate power that is who I really am.

How fascinating the stories of lack and limitation are—and how compellingly they attract our attention! The stories entertain us and fascinate our minds. We have to be brilliant creators to have them appear so compellingly in our lives. And yet if we want to live an enlightened life, we can return to expanded awareness and do our best to find the ultimate truth of our deeper nature—that we are always connected with the Ultimate Reality and that all else is simply a set of stories cast onto the screen of perception.

Our Reality Influences Our Work

All of this profoundly influences the kind of work we do to assist in our own growth and the growth of others. We can "hang around" in the problems till the cows come home, or we can leap into the solution, the connection. On a practical level, we can consistently help ourselves and others to move into more advanced states of consciousness where the remembrance of the infinite reality exists. You can help yourself and others to remember that:

> You are infinitely abundant.
> You are beautiful.
> You are loved and loving.
> You are graced with gifts and talents.
> You are filled with happiness.

Through the Wise Mind Process, you first take the time to explore the limited reality, the apparent problem. Then you release it (through breathing, energy therapies, and other methods that we talk about elsewhere). Then you move into the expanded states where everything is whole and well.

Joy and Happiness in Relationship

Ruth and her partner, James, were walking on a trail together and got into a strong argument. Ruth was feeling guilty for not having worked for two months, and she began to feel insecure with James. As they walked, the heat grew between them, and Ruth was close to turning around and walking back all by herself. Instead, she decided to become aware of what she had created inside herself, and she did the Wise Mind Process.

First she noticed what was going on. She described it: "I want to omit the last thirty minutes from my emotional life completely. As I close my eyes, I allow myself to feel the entire span of my anger and heartache and anxiety. I summon it into me until I feel heaviness in my heart, heat in my head, and a tightening in my gut. I observe all of these physical and emotional sensations, and now I begin to breathe slowly and deeply."

She then continued to breathe: "There is the clean, pure oxygen from the trees that surround me going into my lungs as I inhale, and all the tension and anger is exiting my lungs as I exhale. I visualize the bad feelings as tiny, black spots or germs that float out of my mouth and into the space before me, and as they soar into the sky they break up into a hazy cloud and dissipate into the atmosphere and then into a black hole in space."

She did this for about a minute until she felt completely empty of negative feelings. Then her Wise Mind spoke to her:

> Let the joy of your relationship with James fill your heart. All the negative feelings are coming from your head. They're creations of your imagination, and you can come back to your great love for James. Transform the energy here back in to pure joy and happiness. There is only love.

What happened then was a miracle. She and James began to play—to skip, hop, and run the entire way back to their car. Even their dog began to wag her tail and was in ecstasy the whole time. Ruth was grateful that she could transform her feelings so profoundly and so quickly, and she and James deepened their connection. The love between them was all that mattered.

Any Reality You Like

You have the option to play any game of life that you choose. For the most lasting results, the greatest connection, and the ability to transform the difficulties of life, you can allow your Wise Mind to guide you in remembering the ultimate knowledge of the true nature of your Self.

Chapter Four

Transforming Your Life through the Voice of the Wise Mind

You can't reason yourself out of this
Because your mind is where the problem is in the first place.

—From the film A Beautiful Mind

The question that activates the Wise Mind is, "What would your Wise Mind tell you about that?" I ask this question to every type of person of every age and from every walk of life, and everyone has an answer, for everyone is graced with the good fortune of the Wise Mind. Even people who are taking their first steps in life transformation have answers, and often eloquent ones. I've asked smokers who want to stop, and their Wise Minds show them all the reasons why now is the time. I've asked this question to people with fears, and they instantly tap in to their innate strength and courage. People with anger may tap in to their love. Everyone has an answer. Some answers are elaborate. Other answers are a word, a phrase, or a sentence.

What Is the Wise Mind Like?

The Wise Mind is always positive. If you hear messages
that are negative or critical, that is certainly not the Wise
Mind. It's another nagging voice from a different level of
consciousness. Persevere, and you'll reach the positive
voice. It helps some people to adjust their eyes so that
they look slightly upward. Here is a message one woman,
a mortgage broker, heard. She'd been terrified of speaking
in public. After hearing this voice, she now gives flowing
and captivating talks. Her Wise Mind said to her:

> Be quiet and slow, and say those words as you breathe in
> and out. Keep your mind quiet and slow, and your talk will
> go great. The things you have to say are fascinating to
> people, and they enjoy listening to you. Your talk transmits a
> message. You deliver your message beautifully. Choose
> relaxation. You have everything you need inside of you to
> step into your courage. You have the wisdom of the universe
> within you, and you are an excellent speaker.

The Wise Mind is always encouraging.
It understands that at your core, you're much more
than the concerns of your subterranean selves. It will
always guide you to take the step of courage and to
move into higher levels of your life.

The Wise Mind is often practical.
Surprisingly enough, it will often give you clues
about which fork in the road to take and which to
pass by. Here's what one woman's Wise Mind told
her when she had been harboring great guilt for
planning to leave a relationship that was no longer
working:

You can release your guilt now. You don't need to be guilty about anything. It's not your fault. You're acting from your highest wisdom. Be responsible for yourself, and this will help you to take the best steps. You can feel free to leave now. You're learning something. You will be a lot happier, and so will your partner and everyone else involved.

The Wise Mind is most often spiritual.

Because this is the divine voice implanted in each individual as the personal mirror of the great All That Is, the voice of the Wise Mind will often reflect the transcendent nature of the spiritual fabric from which it is made. One man, a lawyer who carried a great deal of anxiety and insecurity within himself, asked his Wise Mind to tell him whatever it wanted to say. He had perceived himself as having been emotionally and physically abused as a child by a mentally ill father. He always felt that the other shoe was going to drop. Nevertheless, his Wise Mind said:

> That was then; this is now. The purpose of your life is to feel the love of God in your soul. This spirit of love wants you to be happy. The Source of the light is giving the child inside of you love and a feeling of safety. The "I AM" is forever with you. This love is healing all parts of your life.

The Wise Mind is loving.

Because it has its origins in love, it freely and liberally gives that love as a divine benefit to everyone who asks. You can often palpably feel that love when the Wise Mind sends it forth. It opens the heart and sends a rush of healing energy. It can wrap an inner child in its comforting protection. It can fill up the empty spaces that many people have in their hearts, filling those spaces up with nectar that can create states of ecstasy and joy.

The Wise Mind creates possibilities.

It can show you how your current or past experiences have been given to you for your growth and edification. It can convince you to forgive by helping you to have understanding for the other one. It can help you to move on or to hang in there. It can help you move mountains and take you to the next steps in your life. One woman, a graphic designer, was very afraid of the college design class she was going to teach. She did a magnificent job, by the way, as one of the most sought after teachers in the university. Before she got to that step, she wondered if she could do it, and her Wise Mind said to her:

> There's a road you're on. You know you're supposed to be on it. You can't see everything on the road, but you're on it. Trust it. Trusting is the truth. It's okay. The road will just flow. Think of it like a journey. When you look at your hand, remember it's all a dream. Feel faith.

The Wise Mind is brilliant.

The Wise Mind is given to us as our birthright. It's a miracle inside our beings that is activated by our wish to know it. It comes from the spiritual heights and reaches us on our level, uplifting us in the process. All you have to do is ask, "What would my Wise Mind tell me about that?" Then you listen and hear the reply.

Next, you'll read about the Wise Mind Process, a powerful way to transform anything at any moment.

Chapter Five

The Wise Mind Process

By means of the easy and the simple, we grasp the
laws of the whole world.

—The I Ching

Here is a key that can help you transform the dilemmas
of your life easily and deeply and yet is so simple that
even a child can do it. And it's not only simple; it's also
astonishingly profound and effective. And in addition, it
can inspire you to move beyond your troubles into a state
of greater happiness, creativity, and peace. The Wise Mind
Process is a process of transformation that is simple only
at first glance. As you dive more deeply into it, you'll see
the profound ancient roots, and you'll understand why it
reaches into the very core of healing.

We've seen how transformation is different from
change and how it can have a huge impact on everything
you do. Now we'll see how transformation and the Wise
Mind can help you move through perceived challenges in
any aspect of your life. The Wise Mind Process grew out
of my work with many people as well as my own
adventures in self-transformation.

There are some steps you can take even before you

contact the Wise Mind. The Wise Mind Process is based on the inner healing principle of Experience–Release–Transform, which we'll describe in more detail later. The Wise Mind Process is a product of contemporary invention combined with the wisdom of the ages. Based on both Eastern and Western thought, it can help you with fears, pain, negative thoughts, traumas, and much more, and you can use it at any time.

What It's About

The Wise Mind Process has four steps, and each step has a reason and a purpose. Each leads to the next step. Here are the steps:

1. **Pay attention to what is going on inside your body, mind, or emotions. Describe your experience in as much detail as possible.**

2. **Take a deep breath in, and breathe deeply into whatever you're experiencing. As you breathe out, disperse it. Break it up into tiny molecules, and release it into the universe. Do this as many times as you like.**

3. **Ask your Wise Mind what it would like to tell you about this.**

4. **Imagine yourself as you'd like to be. (Pause.) Then find a word or a phrase that symbolizes this. Put your thumb together with your index finger, and say your word or phrase.**

You may want to check to see how you feel and see if

there's anything else you need to pay attention to. See whatever else is needed here for your healing. We'll say more about this later.

This process can be used with eyes open or closed, by professionals and non-professionals alike. It can be used together with whatever else you're already doing, or it can be used instead of what you're doing now. You can use all of the steps together, or you can use one or two or three of the steps individually. Let's take a look at each one of these steps to see what's behind it, and let's see how the process can be used.

Step One:
Pay Attention to What's Happening

One of the greatest ways to transform anything in your life is first to explore and experience what's taking place, especially what's taking place within you. Too often in our society we skip this step. "Go take this purple pill, and you'll obliterate your symptoms." This is what we're told time and time again. Suppress, ignore, or remove your deepest experiences without even looking at them. It is infinitely more effective in the long run, though, to first take a look to see what's there, to see what you've created. How might you describe it? In paying attention to it, you might find that some emotions come up, and that's fine too. You might even find that simply in paying attention, the symptom goes away. You might find that something is taking place within you that you didn't even know was there. This can be a revelation. The monk Thich

Nhat Hanh calls it "looking deeply." It's a necessary step to becoming free.

You might perceive it as tightness in the stomach. It might be sadness in the heart. It might be constricted breathing. Stay with it, describe it, pay attention to it. As you focus on it, you can transform it. You don't dwell on it or become mired in it. You just take the opportunity to pay attention.

Step Two:
Breathe into It, and Exhale It Out

You can take a long, slow breath in, and you imagine that you're breathing that breath directly into your experience of your issue. Your experience might be a pain or a difficult thought or a deep old wound. Breathe into it. Then as you exhale, you imagine that the solidity of the issue changes, and you're breathing your issue out into the Universe, breaking it up into tiny molecules, dispersing it, so it doesn't feel the same within you any longer.

In yoga, many people breathe into the stiffness in their body while doing yoga postures. This can dissolve the tightness and create a new fluidity and flexibility. The practice of breathing in yoga is called pranayama. Prana is the very breath of life itself, the life force in the form of the breath. There is a saying in yoga that "Prana moves chitta." Chitta in Sanskrit means consciousness. And, of course, prana means breath. So breath actually moves consciousness, according to the Sanskrit texts. This means that breathing actually moves matter and thought or awareness. So when you breathe into an issue, you can dissolve it. And when you break it up into tiny molecules, you're changing the structure of the issue. It's simply not the same anymore. You're breaking it up and releasing it into the universe.

In the movie "The Green Mile," Tom Hanks is a prison guard on death row in the Cold Mountain Penitentiary in the Deep South in 1932. A prisoner there named John Coffey, played by Michael Clark Duncan, has been incarcerated for a crime that he didn't commit. He's actually a healer. He can touch something and dissolve it with his touch. He did this one day with the prison guard, Tom Hanks' character, Paul. He reached through the prison bars, touching Paul, and cured him of a recurrent bladder infection. Afterward John began to cough, and soon specks of particulate matter flew out of his mouth to be released into the Universe.

This is similar to the breathing technique that we're talking about in the Wise Mind Process. Break up the issue, and dissolve it into tiny pieces. Let it go.

Step Three:
Ask Your Wise Mind What It Would Like to Tell You about This.

The Wise Mind is brilliant, and it's within everyone, as you already know. The reason for its brilliance is that it's a part of the Infinite Wisdom of the Universe, an actual palpable force that exists in seed form within each being as a birthright. It simply needs to be tapped. The wise force exists in potential in all beings. If you're a healing practitioner and you ask someone, "What would your Wise Mind tell you about this?" you might well be amazed at what comes forth from within people.

Marie perceived that she had difficulties with relationships. She asked her Wise Mind to show her what was in her way. She closed her eyes and saw a seashell. That's all that she could see—a huge shell. She said, "It's blocking me."

Her Wise Mind told her,

> Look closely. You're in that shell.

It felt peaceful in there. Her Wise Mind now had more to say to her:

> You have to come out of your shell, become an ocean. The shell is open now, and there's a pearl in there that's you. You can come out of your shell now. You are the pearl.

Out of her shell! That was it! She saw it, she felt it, she knew what was blocking her, and as she began to explore the pearl, she had a good direction in which to go. Her Wise Mind had spoken to her in a visual metaphor, and not only was she shown the way out, but she was also given the experience of the next step, the expansion of her life.

Step Four:
Imagine Yourself as You'd Like to Be. (Pause.) Then Find a Healing Word or Phrase, and Anchor It with Your Thumb and Index Finger

Step Four activates the potential that lies inside in seed form and opens you to what you're becoming. To be able to have a hand in giving this potential shape and form is the art of conscious manifestation. While there's something to be said for just being in the "now," it is still dynamically valuable to be able to birth a new vision for yourself, your life, and the world on the level of the deep inner mind. It's a way to realize what's possible for you.

Step Four is also a perfect way to reclaim the power in yourself that has been hiding under the limitations of your old way of being. As you release and transform what was, you reclaim your power. You may imagine yourself as behaving in a new way or having something you've wished for—or you can imagine yourself as a radiantly powerful being of enlightenment and joy.

After you activate this potential by imagining yourself as you'd like to be, you "anchor" it with a word or phrase. This anchoring step owes its power to NLP or neurolinguistic programming. The premise is that if you do something (like touch a shoulder or finger) at the time of a positive experience, you can condition yourself or another to have a positive experience when you do the same thing again in another situation. This is taken from Pavlov's experiment in operant conditioning in which he had dogs salivate at the sound of a bell. You don't necessarily want to salivate, but you can create a positive response by linking the desired state with something like a touch or image.

Anchoring is like pressing the "save" key on your computer. The act of touching the thumb together with the index finger is also like making the "okay" sign. In addition, it's called a mudra in yoga, in which the individual will of the finger touches the divine will of the thumb. What we're doing in the Wise Mind Process is anchoring the healing with words and touch. It's really quite simple, and it can create powerful results.

If You Like, Find Anything Else That Needs to Be Done to Heal

Check in and see if there's anything else to do. You can always do the Wise Mind Process over and over again. You can also add more to it.

Some questions you might ask are:

- Does the inner child need to be attended to?

- Is there still some discomfort in the body?

- Is there anything that needs to be communicated?

- Are there still some feelings that need to be felt and understood?

- Is it necessary to find any history or root cause?

- Anything else at all?

If anything else comes up, you can do this again, as I've mentioned, and you can also add other approaches, such as EFT tapping (see my book *Extraordinary Healing* for more information on tapping), inner child love, regression, or anything else that seems as if it would be helpful.

You can do the Wise Mind Process over again as many times as you'd like. You can do it in an office, in a car, in your house, with a mouse, in a box, with a fox, with a goat, on a boat—with Dr. Seuss or with yourself. Enjoy its power and see how it might help you overcome the challenges of life. It's amazingly simple, yet it works, and you can use it for all the issues of your life.

As you read on, you'll find out about someone who changed every aspect of her life and the life of her family with the brilliant power of the great Wise Mind.

Chapter Six

A Story of Grace and the Wise Mind

Your pain is the breaking of the shell that encloses your understanding.

—Kahlil Gibran, *The Prophet*

Grace never had a feeling of being loved. She carried this around in her heart, and it affected everything she did. She now had a good family, a husband and two teenage children, but inside herself there was an empty hole in her heart. She'd always tell herself, "Everyone's going to get it but me—health, success, money. Good things pass me by, and others get them."

The main problem, as Grace perceived it, was that she had never felt loved by her mother. Her mother had herself felt abandoned and alone. She lashed out at people because she was wrapped up in a blanket of fear, anger, and unhappiness. If her mother had a headache, she'd think it was a brain tumor, and even though she had excellent health, the atmosphere around her was studded with an all-pervasive sense of gloom and doom. This was, of course, Grace's version of reality. In truth, she wasn't connected with the love inside herself, and everything in her life was a reflection of that.

Grace had been a very sensitive little girl, and she always wanted her mother to love her. She craved feeling secure, and in wishing to be loved and nurtured, she became the "good girl" who tried and tried to get her mother to be kind to her. Nothing worked. Everyone thought she was balanced and healthy, but inside she had the hole in her heart that she wanted to fill with love. She criticized herself and told herself to "get over it already." She sought counseling and wrote in many journals. She concentrated on her husband and children and acted as if everything were okay.

She tried to heal herself through counseling, but her strong thoughts were too much in the way. "I don't deserve good in my life. I'll never accomplish things. I feel like a failure." She kept waiting for something drastic to happen, and she'd find herself imagining the worst.

Grace Begins to Transform Her Mind and Her Life

Grace was introduced to the Wise Mind Process, and the first step was to describe her experience. She had always danced around her grief, never allowing herself to actually pay attention to it. She finally looked at it, and she saw it as an experience of living under a gray cloud that always held the promise of sun that never truly appeared. Her secret fear was that if she truly felt the grief in its dark entirety, then she would explode into a thousand tiny pieces, and she'd never be whole again. This was how unsafe she felt. So she was truly surprised when she was asked to breathe into her experience and imagine it breaking into tiny pieces as she then sent the pieces off into the universe. At first it was a challenging thing to do, but she soon realized that she wasn't going to be broken up into the tiny pieces; her grief was. The moment she realized this marked the beginning of her transformation.

Her Wise Mind told her,

> **You deserve all the peace, security, and love you've always wanted.**

She realized that at a very deep level, her mother indeed loved her but was unable to show it due to her own limitations. Grace's inner wisdom pointed the way toward a compassionate detachment. She sensed a profound feeling of self-love she had never experienced before. She felt complete. She imagined herself as radiant and beaming. She anchored this new phenomenon with the words "My mother's love resides in my heart." She had transformed that dark ball of pain, which had always lurked in her heart.

Grace Continues On with the Process and Finds More Love

One day Grace felt a pain in her pelvis where she'd once had a cyst. "Oh, my God, it's a tumor!" would have been her old panicky way of reacting to such things. She had some of the same thoughts, but now she was able to observe them without the same panic or anxiety. A few thoughts came up: "Maybe this is terminal. What if my kids grow up without me and have to go to my funeral?" She just observed the thoughts and stayed with the

feelings. She did the Wise Mind Process. She used to push
such feelings away, but not now. She sat with them,
breathed through them, and she released them. She asked
her Wise Mind what it was trying to teach her. And her
Wise Mind showed her important things:

> Have love and compassion for yourself. You don't have to be
> so hard on yourself. Accept yourself where you're at, and
> really trust in the process of life. You can be healthy and
> heal yourself. You're healing yourself with love. You deserve
> this love. You've given all your love to your children. Now
> you can be kind and loving to yourself. You have all the love
> you need to heal yourself.

She felt a sense of great well-being and calmness. She
felt great love in her heart and wisdom in her mind.

Grace Heals Her Relationship
with Her Husband

On the surface everything had been great with her
husband, James. But underneath the aura of perfection
lurked Grace's heart, which was not fully open to him. It
had started a number of years ago when James had had
business difficulties, which had alienated him from
Grace's parents and, to a much lesser extent, from Grace
as well. She stayed by him, but she never fully gave her
heart to him. Grace wanted her parents' love, and she also
wanted things to go well with James, so she'd been pulled
in two directions. Even though it wasn't logical, she had
some pain and anger toward him. He was "going to take
care" of her, and he "blew it." When the Wise Mind
Process came into her life, Grace broke open the closed

vault of her heart. As feelings would come up, her Wise Mind would tell her,

Forgiveness is healing you. Trust in the power of love.

She hadn't made eye contact with James for many years, and now she looked right at him. She asked him, "Did you get new glasses?" "Yes," he said, "five years ago." She remembered what brought them together, and she now still looks into his entire face.

James himself has opened up. He realized that he'd been very shut down throughout his ordeals—and throughout his entire life. But he's done the Wise Mind Process too, and though it's harder for him to feel his feelings, he's opened up. He believes in himself again, and that's a very great step.

Grace's Son Has a Breakthrough

Steven had terrible anxiety about taking tests. He allowed his mom to introduce him to the Wise Mind Process. His Wise Mind told him,

You know this material. You don't need to be afraid. You can be confident.

His special word was "relax." He felt completely relaxed the day of his test, and he continues to improve in school.

Grace Talks about the Process

"This has given me a tool I'll continue to use throughout my life," Grace says. "I'll share it with others. It has been life altering. For me, it takes things out of the head and puts them into the heart. I've kept journals since age twenty, about my feelings of low self-esteem and self-worth. I saw myself repeating the same patterns over and over. The Wise Mind Process has transformed it all from my head to my heart. I feel different. I feel calm, and even in those moments when I don't, I have the tools to trust what's inside. I trust my inner wisdom, and my life has been transformed."

Chapter Seven

More on Step One:
Describing Your Situation, Paying Attention

*Recognize what is in your sight, and what is hidden
will come clear to you.*

—Jesus, in the Gospel of Thomas

The act of describing has great power. If you perceive a
pain in your body, such as a headache, you can describe it,
noticing its shape and weight and color, and as you
describe it you may notice that it shifts and often
ultimately disappears. The art of observation can work
miracles. As you observe, you may see surface qualities, or
you may see more deeply. You might say something like,
"Yes, I notice this rapid breathing in my chest as my
anxiety. I have it whenever I'm asked to perform in any
way. It reminds me of when I was twelve and had to
perform in school. Now I notice my breathing is much
less rapid. It's calming down, and so am I."

Paying attention is about observing your own mind and
emotions—in no way rejecting them, just watching. The
moment you watch yourself, you leap into a more
expanded state called the witness state. Even though in

this first step you're describing your difficulties, you're also observing them, and that takes you another step toward liberation from your difficulties.

The teachings of mindfulness, a Buddhist practice, are about paying attention. The moment we do it, everything changes. Thich Nhat Hanh, the gentle and deep Buddhist monk, writes about mindfulness in many of his books. In his groundbreaking, best-selling book *Peace Is Every Step*, he says, "The first step in dealing with feelings is to recognize each feeling as it arises. The agent that does this is mindfulness. In the case of fear, for example, you bring out your mindfulness, look at your fear, and recognize it as fear." [ii]

Most of the time we want to just get rid of things. We tell them to go away, as if we're waving off a small child or a pesky neighbor. But it works better to acknowledge things, and then we can transform them. Remember that transformation is about shifting things, not getting rid of them. This is a significant difference. Milarepa, the great yogi, had his own way of dealing with this. He was on a retreat, and he returned to his cave after gathering firewood one day. There he observed many demons, and he told them over and over that they had to go away. He yelled at them and swatted at them. One particular demon wouldn't leave, and finally the monk sighed and said to him, "Okay, stay for a while, and we can have some tea together. We'll talk about the teachings." At that very moment, the demon said, "Goodbye!" and left him forever. That was a great moment of transformation.

The Guest House in Your Soul

Rumi, the great Sufi poet, had wisdom and heart as large as the cosmos. His poems ring out truths that even centuries after they were written are still profoundly meaningful. Rumi wrote about the growth of the soul, about transcendence and metamorphosis. One of his poems about tending to and healing the emotions is particularly relevant. He says that every person is a guest house. Every day emotions and feelings come in as unexpected visitors. He tells us to "welcome and entertain them all"—every joy, depression, meanness, shame, or malice. Rumi guides us to welcome these guests, even if they're "sweeping your house out of all its furniture." He says that maybe a "guest" is clearing you out for some "new delight." Rumi says that guests are "guides from beyond," and we need to give some attention to them, inviting them in.

Rumi is telling us that inviting in rather than locking out or rejecting the experiences that we create on a regular basis will open us to all the experiences of our life. It's about perceiving illness and pain as both illusions and guests. If you don't pay attention to your wife or husband, your child, your friend, your fear, or your sadness, the problems can escalate. Again, in our culture we like to push things down, get rid of them, banish them, drug them into the oblivion of unconsciousness, but here we're being invited to welcome them all into a guest house. If we suppress our feelings, they keep popping back up, like jack-in-the-boxes. If we pay attention to them, just like human beings, they are magically comforted, soothed, and transformed.

What You Might Observe

You pay attention to the way your body feels. You notice thought forms that arise. You watch patterns of breathing. You see if any previous experiences wish to present themselves to you. You remain as present in the moment with this experience as you possibly can. You explore whatever you're experiencing in your deep inner mind.

You may find tightness in your chest or a pain somewhere. You may find that your breathing is shallow or that a thought springs up out of the blue. You may find tears coming or anger rising to the surface. Whatever it is, you just pay attention. It's about becoming centered and creating a bridge to awareness.

Let's say you had a fear of driving across bridges. You might describe it like this, "My heart is beating fast, and my hands are moist. My throat is choked up, and my feet feel as if they're rising up off the ground. My mouth is dry, and I feel as if I'd like to go under the covers instead of drive across that bridge."

You might ask for more details: "I fear that my car will go over the side of that bridge if I lose control. I fear losing control because I've had these symptoms before, and they were debilitating."

You continue to observe: "My father comes to mind. He practically came unglued when he was teaching me to drive. His terror was infectious."

And then you ask yourself, "Is there anything else here I need to know?" You look even more deeply, and you perceive within yourself a tiny child who feels all alone. Where is everyone? No one is there.

The First Step

So this is the first step in the Wise Mind Process of self-transformation. It can be detailed as in the example above. It can also be brief. It is about coming to know what you're creating on whatever level inside your being. It may involve old pictures and feelings and thoughts of times past; it may be entirely focused on the moment.

The ancient and wise Lao Tzu said in the *Tao Te Ching*, his book of poetic verses:

> In standing back
> from your own mind
> you begin to understand all things

One of the things he is talking about here is the art of being the witness, of standing back and observing your own experience. It works to remind yourself that there is no absolute reality in what you're experiencing, that you're making it up in your mind and feelings. This gives you perspective as you allow yourself to feel and experience whatever you perceive is there.

The Subterranean Inner World

So Lao Tzu asks us if we can stand back and allow the inner workings of things to unfold. You can move back a bit, "stand back from your own mind." You allow your own inner mind to reveal a brilliant database of material that has its own rhyme and reason, its own logic. With this attitude of deep interest, you can see what's taking place in this subterranean inner world. You ask yourself the leading questions, and much is revealed. Here are some of the possible questions:

- What's happening here?

- Who is there?

- What am I feeling, seeing, hearing, knowing?

- Is there anything else I need to know?

- Tell me more.

- Does this remind me of any previous experience, and do I need to know what it might be?

- Where do I feel this in my body?

- How am I picturing this or representing it in my mind?

- Is there a particular part of me that is in need of healing?

- Tell me more.

You can approach this with your intuitive and spiritual powers, or you can be primarily scientific and pragmatic.

Your experiences might come as symbols. You might experience an empty warehouse in which you're alone and there's no furniture. This may be symbolic of the alienation you feel. Or you might experience a great light that is a foreshadowing of the illumination you're preparing to experience in greater fullness.

Hard Work or Ease

The Wise Mind Process may come easily to you. It may take some practice. Some people can ice-skate or dance effortlessly. For you, it may come naturally or it may take a while. You may want to write down all that you're discovering. You may want to talk to another about your findings.

Eventually you become adept at standing back and viewing your own mind, seeing from the state of witness consciousness. Again, as Lao Tzu says: "In standing back from your own mind, you begin to understand all things."

Chapter Eight

More on Step Two: Breathing and Breaking Up Your Issue into Tiny Molecules

When we inhale, the air comes into the inner world.
When we exhale, the air goes out to the outer world.
The inner world is limitless, and the outer world is also limitless. . . .
Actually, there is just one whole world.

—Shunryu Suzuki, *The Enlightened Mind*

The breath has the capacity to ease pain and soften tension. When you concentrate on breathing, your mind is able to gather together all its scattered energies. Your mind becomes much more focused, quiet, and clear. In fact, when you focus on your breathing, you are in the present, in the here and now. You are able to truly shift from one state of consciousness to another.

The Breath Moves Consciousness

In chapter 2 we introduced the extraordinary idea that the breath has the power to actually move matter and consciousness to new states of being. Again, prana is the Sanskrit word for life force, the very energy of the universe, and pranayama is the practice of controlling that force. The life force is manifested in many forms, one of which is the breath. When we focus on breathing, we focus on directing the life force within us. Remember prana moves consciousness. Pranayama focuses and quiets your mind and helps you move energy. That's why it's so powerful to breathe into your perceived difficulties. It moves them, shifts them, transforms them.

Rapid, Anxious Breathing

Notice your breathing when you feel anxious and uncentered. It's high up in your chest, and it's shallow and rapid. Some people feel as if their feet are going to leave the ground. Others break out into pronounced sweats. Rapid breathing and fear thoughts can create the perception of anxiety.

By breathing more deeply and bringing your breath down into your belly, you'll feel a greater sense of peace. Breathing into your issue and breathing out, dispersing your issue by breaking it up into tiny molecules, deeply transforms your life experiences.

Constricted Breathing

When you open and relax your breathing, you're able to release and transform old habits of mind with greater ease. The Buddha said, "Being sensitive to the whole body, the yogi breathes in; being sensitive to the whole body, the yogi breathes out."[iii]

Breaking Up Your Issue into Tiny Molecules

Great wisdom throughout all the ages has pointed to a profound fact: that reality is not as solid as it seems. In fact, we don't see things the way they actually are. The book *A Course in Miracles* asks us to look at a table and see that we're not seeing it in its true form. We think it's solid, yet it is made up of the very fluid energy of the universe itself. We've created a reality that is separate from the truth of our oneness with All That Is. In fact, we think our challenges are solid, and they appear daunting to us. But when we break them up into tiny molecules, the solidity dissolves, and we now have the opportunity to experience the transformation of our issues more easily.

Reality in Quantum Physics

In the same way, in quantum physics we're invited to understand the universe as composed of minute strings that are in constant motion. According to string theory, if we could examine these particles, we would find each string consists of a tiny, one-dimensional loop. Like an infinitely thin rubber band, each particle contains a vibrating, oscillating, dancing filament that physicists have named a string. To many quantum physicists, this is what underlies all matter. So things are not as solid as they seem. Yet even the strings are nevertheless illusory, as all that really exists is consciousness and love.

The Vedas, the Upanishads, Kashmir Shaivism, and Kabbalah

Many ancient spiritual texts also discuss the nature of reality, and they too say that the world we perceive with our senses is not the ultimate reality. They may use the word maya to point to the limited and finite world, and some of them speak of Brahman as the pure oneness of all creation. Here, we're working toward returning to the consciousness of supreme bliss by dissolving the solidity of our perceptions step by step and returning home to the "real." From *The Upanishads* comes this great prayer:

> Lead us from darkness into light,
> From the unreal to the real,
> Om shanti, shanti, shanti.
> Om peace, peace, peace.

There is a great ancient cosmology called Kashmir Shaivism. As you may have guessed, it comes from Kashmir, near India and Pakistan, in the eighth or ninth century, and it has to do with Shiva, another name for the Great Spirit. It diagrams a great movement of consciousness from full awareness to the most limited forms of negativity and strife. In the beginning was the great Oneness. Then over time, blinders began to hide the truth, and limited understanding and emotions such as greed, ignorance, and ego became given realities. Experiences became solidified. The task then is to desolidify the appearances of reality and come back to what is truly real.

Fascinatingly enough, many other traditions understand the universe through the same cosmology. This includes the Kabbalah, the Sufi texts, the Rosicrucians, the Buddhists, and many more. The Kabbalah speaks of the emanation or unfolding of steadily denser planes or spheres from the spiritual summit. Everything has divinity as its nature, and everything is a movement back toward uniting the higher and lower worlds once again.

The One Remains; the Many Change and Pass

To transform this through the Wise Mind Process, you break up your reality into tiny molecules and disperse them into the universe as you dissolve the solidity of your reality and return to truth again. This is the work of true transformation and the path that all of us are traveling on. As we shift and dissolve the solid nature of our perceived suffering, we find that we can more easily enter a reality that is filled with wisdom, love, and light.

As Shelley, the great poet, said:

> The One remains, the many change and pass;
> Heaven's light forever shines, Earth's shadows fly;
> Life, like a dome of many-colour'd glass,
> Stains the white radiance of eternity. [iv]

Chapter Nine

More on Step Three: The Wise Mind

*Without beginning or ending, your original wisdom
has been shining forever, like the sun. . . .*

*When you realize that all phenomena are as unstable
as the air, they lose their power to fascinate and bind you. . . .*

*Look into the true state, where self-awareness, self-knowledge,
self-illumination shine resplendently. This is called the enlightened mind.*

—Padmasambhava, from The Book of the Great Liberation

As we've been saying, the Wise Mind is one aspect of higher consciousness. Other aspects are love, peace, light, and compassion. The Wise Mind is a part of the superconscious, and everyone has the capacity to experience it when the conscious mind becomes quiet. The Wise Mind is the voice of the Universal Self as it speaks through you. It is the great macrocosm, the whole expressing itself through the microcosm that is you.

Most of our ills are caused by a lack of connection with the superconscious state, yet everyone has the ability to make this contact. The only things in the way for some people are the blinders that they wear, which prevent them from even looking. These illusory blinders are doubt, ignorance, inner darkness, emotional chaos, or the myriad of perceived traumas and wounds that keep people from looking toward the inner gifts.

What Can the Wise Mind Tell Us?

The Wise Mind is crucially important to the healing process because it can shift your view of your own reality. Doing this can lift you out of dark places and misconceptions in a matter of moments. The "Wise Mind" is the higher faculty of advanced consciousness, wisdom, or guidance that is innate in the human organism. Through it, you bring forth experiences that arise from an inner source. "What would my Wise Mind tell me about this?" is a life-altering question. Perhaps your Wise Mind would like to tell you what an entire experience in your life has meant to your growth. It may show you an answer to a dilemma. It may give you ancient wisdom to put your own situation in perspective. It may show you a way of living your life that puts you on a more fruitful path. Connecting with the Wise Mind is an ancient art. The healing temples of ancient Greece and Rome are perfect examples.

The Ancient Healing Temples

The ancient healing temples of Greece and Rome are fascinating forerunners of our current transformational paradigm. These great temples are one of the predecessors of modern healing. There was an extraordinary order of priest-physicians around 1200 to 1000 BC. Their great leader was Aesclepius, and their accomplishments were miraculous. When Aesclepius died, temples dedicated to him were often built near healing waters, like the spas of today. The temples were places of beauty and sacred dignity.

In these healing temples, patients were diagnosed and treated according to dream experiences that they had there. They would come to the temples and be prepared for the healing process. They'd be clothed in white garments, and they were brought onto couches, where they were instructed to dream a healing dream. In the morning the patients told their healing dream to the priest-physicians, who then prepared the herbal formulas for them. Amazingly, the patients recovered. Blind people recovered their eyesight. Scars were removed. A boy recovered his speech. People were cured of all kinds of ailments.

The Medicine That Exists Inside

Like the ancient ones, we too acknowledge that there is an inner "medicine" that we can find within ourselves. We can find answers in the deep resources of our inner mind. We recognize the wealth of information that lies in the Wise Mind, and we can honor what comes forth as the rich material of deepest being. In this sense, we are our own priest-physicians.

Communication from the Wise Mind

Rachel was growing daily in her consciousness, and she began to feel fear and guilt because she thought she was going to create a rift with her husband. She said, "I should do things to bring us and keep us together, and instead I'm growing by leaps and bounds." She created a lot of "shoulds" to limit herself. Nevertheless, doors were opening in her awareness, and she asked her Wise Mind to speak to her:

> There's divine harmony in everything. As your soul is called upon to grow, there's also a perfect next step for your husband and everyone in your family. By stepping into the alignment of your souls, you allow others in your life to step into their higher soul purpose as well. Let yourself feel increasing joy in all you do.

Everything in your life is an opportunity for awakening. Everything has the potential for transformation. The Wise Mind often indicates the significance of particular experiences in our lives and invites us to move into a new dimension of understanding. God spoke to Jeremiah and said, "Call to Me, and I will . . . show you great things . . . which you do not know" (Jeremiah 33:3). Ask the Wise Mind a question, and the doorway to life transformation will open up to you.

Chapter Ten

More on Step Four: Imagining Yourself as You'd Like to Be and Anchoring It

Each of us has one or more talents we love to express.
When we are fully and freely expressing who we really are, we feel
joyful and fulfilled. The more love we feel for ourselves, the more
we allow the creative energy of the Universe to flow through us.

—*Arnold Patent, The Journey*

By imagining yourself as you'd like to be, you send out a broadcast of what you'd like for your life in the outer, visible, tangible world. You experience this plan in its finished form—an act of sending out to the universe a powerful message about your next step. Both the activity of inner seeing or feeling and your power to create are attributes of your greatest Self, all of which are inherent in the very core of your being. Imagination is a miraculous force, and life is the images of your mind expressed. You live the life that you've imagined.

Thoughts and feelings, as we know, have extraordinary power. They have vibrational and creative potency in them, and so imagining yourself as you'd like to be is an act of life planning and deep rehearsal. It is a message sent to the universe that the content of your thoughts is determining the next phase as well as the quality of your life.

Here is your opportunity to remember the infinitely powerful being that is your true nature. Through the process of transformation, you have uncovered a small rock or a large boulder under which your infinite power lies. Now your power is revealed to you, and you are able to move forward into the next phase of your life.

Anchoring Your Aspiration for Your Life

When you'd like to moor a boat, you throw down an anchor. When you'd like to save your work on your computer, you press "save." In the Wise Mind Process, anchoring is used to save the healing information that you've received. Later on you can retrieve this information by reproducing your anchor. In the Wise Mind Process, you find a healing word or phrase (or even a visual image) that symbolizes what you're creating for your life. Then you put your thumb together with your index finger and say the word or phrase to yourself. The principle behind this is that every time you do and say your word or phrase, you can come back to the transformed experience, no matter where you are.

In the same way that Pavlov's dogs were conditioned to salivate at the sound of the bell by associating food with the bell, the principle here is that you associate your transformation with your word or phrase and the position of your fingers.

Origins of Anchoring

The concept of anchoring comes from NLP, neurolinguistic programming, originated by Richard Bandler and John Grinder in the 1970s. Tony Robbins is also well known for his use of anchoring. One of the best ways to reinforce positive states is by associating a particular action with a positive state. Triggering that action will bring it forth, and that's the basis of anchoring.

Some "Wise Mind Process" Anchors

Amy had a habitual tendency to put herself down, to feel insecure, and to find herself put down by others. Paying attention to it, she found knots in her stomach and tightness in many places in her body. Her Wise Mind showed her a bird of freedom taking away her burdens. She felt light and free. She imagined herself as radiant and centered, and she put her thumb together with her index finger, saying, "I am lightness." This is something she can do consistently in the context of her life to continue to maintain her centered state.

Janice perceived great childhood pain and sadness. In paying attention, she felt the sadness throughout her body, as she braced herself for something terrible to happen and always waited for the other shoe to drop. Her Wise Mind showed her the great resource she had for transforming this sadness: the love of her grandmother (which triggered her own experience of love). She imagined herself experiencing the great comfort of her grandmother's presence. She put her thumb together with her index finger and experienced herself together with her grandmother as she said, "I am loved." The experience of love is the central healing resource that is innate in everyone, and it manifests in one form or another. It's highly significant, as the lack of this connection with the high vibration of love is the primary cause of all human emotional difficulties, and it can be called forth through an anchor, a powerful healing tool.

Still one more woman, Anita, had a paralyzing fear of going to the dentist. She paid attention to a feeling of panic, like she might pass out. She remembered a dentist from when she was ten, a man who'd been cruel and who'd hurt her, and she'd held onto this perception ever since. Her Wise Mind gave her two angels—one of Courage and one of Peace. She imagined herself in the dentist's chair in a state of bliss. She anchored with her thumb and index finger, seeing the angels and saying the words, "courage and peace." Her next visit to a dentist was ecstatic and beautiful. She was also able to shift her consciousness to a state of comfort and peace.

It would be ideal if all you had to do were to do this once and it would last forever. That can happen, but sometimes patterns recur. As you meet them with awareness and perseverance, you build your experience of transformation and enlightenment step by step.

The Thumb and the Index Finger

Together the thumb and index finger create the "okay" sign—and yet they do much more. If you've looked at a sculpture or painting from India, Tibet, China, Korea, or Japan, the spiritual figures in them often hold their hands in certain positions. The thumb together with the index finger is one we see often. These hand positions are called mudras. Mudras are positions of the body that have particular types of influences on the energies of your body or on your mood. For spiritual figures, such hand positions are believed to generate forces that invoke the sacred.

The gesture of thumb and the index finger pressed together creates calming and enhances happiness; it also improves concentration and intellect. It's very grounding, and it's the symbol of the Universal will in harmony with the individual will.

Carrying the Anchor into Your Life

When working with your deepest issues, it's important to have something to carry into daily life to reinforce the transformed experience. This is why having a tangible anchoring experience can be very helpful as a reminder, in addition to the rest of the Wise Mind Process.

As you read on, you'll find out about the transformation of my own ability to speak the truth.

Chapter Eleven

The Bonus Step:
Anything Else That Needs to Be Transformed?

Quiet the outgoing mental restlessness
And turn the mind within. . . .
Then you will see the underlying harmony in your life and in all nature.

—*Paramahansa Yogananda*

For so long I'd perceived myself as beset with deep fears of speaking in public, particularly fears of speaking on the radio. This was fascinating because it was something I did quite often. I sat with myself, and I asked the questions, paying attention to my situation, as I truly wanted to speak my truth.

I paid attention to my experience: "My legs are shaking; my feet feel as if they're going to leave the ground; my breathing is so shallow, I can hardly take another breath. I feel paralyzed and tongue-tied. I've felt this since sixth grade, when someone laughed at me during a piano recital. I know I'm creating this in my own mind, as I know I have something to say." I breathed into it and breathed it out.

"What would my Wise Mind tell me about this?" I asked myself. "You can do this," my Wise Mind told me.

You are now being inspired and assisted by something larger than yourself. I AM here to assist you. Just tune in to this force beyond you, and you'll do beautifully. As you do it more and more, you'll have familiarity with it. You'll do it with ease. Tune in to what you're saying and what your purpose is. Step out of your ego, and speak from your soul. Speak from a clear state.

"Is there anything more I need to know?" I asked my Wise Mind. I went inside myself to my experience as a young girl at a piano recital. I was playing "Hungarian Dance No. 5," and another little girl was dancing to it. When I made mistakes, the little dancing girl grimaced and groaned. As I perceived it, the audience found it hilarious. I heard my father's booming voice laughing, and I felt my own humiliation. I brought love and compassion to myself as a girl. I was instantly relieved. The Laughing Buddha appeared before me, laughing with hilarity and sheer joy. The Buddha said to me, "So what? Let them laugh, and you can laugh as well!" I felt a new energy come into my body and mind, and an uplifted state—almost a state of grace, in which I knew that a force beyond myself was with me at each moment. I was also given a technique to use. I put my thumb together with my index finger on both hands, and I said to myself, "All systems go!" I noticed a channel of energy come down through my head, to indicate to me that I was allowing the words to come through me naturally and spontaneously. I could be a channel for the healing power of the Universe. This took me out of my own personal self and allowed me to go beyond my own limitations to a more expanded state of being. In truth, I created the entire experience in order to give myself the opportunity to transform. Because I made it all up, I could recreate it any way I chose. There is nothing outside of me, and I have the ability to expand my experiences of reality at any moment.

Doing Something More

You may feel you need to take another step or two to resolve an issue. As we've seen in chapter 2, you can always do the Wise Mind Process over and over again. You can also add more to it:

- Do you feel that the child within you needs to be attended to?

- You may want to ask yourself how old is the one who's having the experience you're describing. If it's a child, you may want to find out what's happening and what that part of you needs. Usually the need is for love, and you can bring love to that child in any number of ways. Again, whatever you perceive about the child is not the true reality, though it is often helpful to bring love and comfort. Love is the true energy of the universe, and any time it is remembered, it brings resolution and joy.

- Is there any other part of you that requires your attention?

There are illusory characters, children and adults, happy and sad, bold and scared, inside of us, in what I call "frozen pictures in the soul." Though they are seemingly from the past, we can become aware of them in the here and now, in this very moment. It's often a life-transforming event to find these "beings" inside of us. In many ways they've been asking us to pay attention to them. We create incidents and experiences similar to our past experiences so that we can heal them. We all have these pictures, and it is possible to find them. In the same way that we capture moments in our photo albums, so too we capture moments in the deep inner mind, and the inner characters in these moments help to shape our behaviors and thoughts. There may be a small teenage boy, teased by the others, who now questions his strength. There may be a girl who, when molested, froze in a state of shock, anger, and fear—so much that her current relationships are strained. There may be a mother who lost her children and who remains in a state of perpetual grief. Once retrieved and paid attention to, all these beings can be awakened, recognized, loved, soothed, and healed. The truth of the matter, however, is that these inner beings have no real existence, and as we come more and more into the truth of the superconscious mind, the old pictures cease to have power.

• Is there still some discomfort in your body?

This too may be a deeper issue that's seeking resolution by manifesting in physical ways.

• Is there anything that needs to be communicated?

Is there some undelivered communication that is sitting inside of you? Is there something you'd like to tell someone? If so, it might be helpful to voice it either to yourself or aloud, as it can remove the burden from your system.

• Are there still some feelings that need to be felt and understood?

Do you need to understand the feelings involved more

fully? If so, can you describe your experience even more deeply?

• Is it necessary to find any history or root cause?

If possible, you may want to see if you can find an antecedent for the experience you're having now. The reality, however, is that the true cause of most of our ills is separation from the universal Self. So if you can go that high, that far, and that deep, you'll no doubt take yourself to a root of a situation. If you'd like to stay in the current reality, you may be able to find an experience that has set your current pattern in motion.

• Anything else at all?

If anything else comes up, you can do the Wise Mind process again, and you can also add other approaches, such as EFT tapping, regression, or anything else that seems as if it would be helpful. You'll find a great deal more about this in my book *Extraordinary Healing.*[v]

Going More Deeply

Jordan had intense stomach cramps. He'd been getting them regularly for the past three days. He described them: "It feels like there's an intense squeezing inside my gut, from the pit of my stomach down." He remembered a very early time when he felt the same way. "I was in third grade, age eight, and I can picture it vividly. I see myself sitting in my classroom. My teacher is very strict, and I have stomachaches as she's criticizing me. I hear her saying, 'You didn't understand the assignment. You read the wrong thing!' My stomach hurts a lot."

Jordan breathed into it and released it. His Wise Mind said to him,

> It's really not so bad. Don't take it personally. Criticism is designed to make you stronger. Work even harder, and you'll do even better. It's your "trial by fire," and through it, you're transforming. The past experience is over. It's not even real. You're way beyond that now.

He imagined himself as powerful, as his posture straightened and his stomach relaxed. His word was "confident."

He got it, yet there was something more he wanted and needed to do. It was important to him to pay more attention to that eight-year-old boy. He imagined his present self going to the boy and giving him reassurance, confidence. He put his arm around him and told him he was growing way beyond this, and he told him that he loved him.

The fascinating part of this was that Jordan's eight-year-old son had started third grade that morning. Jordan had been the target of his estranged wife's criticism as well, and these "recurrent similars" were triggering the old symptoms. This was, of course, his perfect opportunity to heal, and now he was able to leap across time and space and heal that fragile part of himself that was an antecedent to his current troubling experiences. Jordan was relieved, and his face radiated a huge smile.

This is valuable inner transformation. When we adopt a welcoming and allowing attitude to all of our experiences, we can go beyond condemnation, shame, and judgment, and we can find an expanded attitude of embracing what comes, which can only serve to expand and enlighten us.

Chapter Twelve

Experience–Release–Transform

The soul is the home of all living beings,
And from the soul, all living beings derive their strength.

—The Upanishads

The Wise Mind Process follows a flow that is reflected in most of the transformational work that we do. It's a series of stages through which the healing naturally moves. Those stages are: Experience–Release–Transform.

When you look at the Wise Mind Process, you see that in Step One, you're experiencing and paying attention to your issue. In Step Two, you're breathing and releasing it. In Step Three, you're transforming it through the vehicle of the Wise Mind.

Experience

Experiencing what's going on within you is, in its own way, an art form—the art of paying attention. Paying attention to places in which you're hiding your power under old limitations helps you to transform those limitations into freedom and joy.

Release

Release, the second step, is a natural process. Clouds release raindrops when it's time to let the rain come. Boils on the skin release foreign matter when it's time to heal. Mothers (hopefully) release their children when it's time for them to grow up. And so do we release old issues when it's time for us to let go. Sometimes we do it vocally; sometimes we do it energetically. Sometimes the release is visual. Breathing is a powerful way to release.

Transform

The third step, transformation, comes when you're ready to shift your consciousness to a new level, when you are ready to see with different eyes. The enlightened ones remind us that we're asleep and dreaming this reality. It seems so real, yet your Wise Mind can lead you to great expanded realities and new areas of understanding. Sometimes the transformation will take you to places suffused with light. Or you may experience a profound wisdom coming forth that is way beyond your usual ability to be wise. You may find that deep understanding is flowing from your soul. Always, you will be uplifted into the experience of love.

The Transformational Process

This transformational process is a natural one. We may have the perception that everything is constantly transforming in the universe. After the rain, the dust of the city is cleaned away. The air is fresh, and you may perceive a kind of purity in the atmosphere. In the Wise Mind Process, you create this transformation in a microcosmic way, in the twinkling of an eye. You go through the steps of Experience–Release–Transform, and you bring yourself back to your natural state of healing, wisdom, and love. You bring every molecule and cell back to the consciousness of the One.

"Everything is made of

the stuff of higher consciousness,

and if you can see this with your own eyes,

you can lead an uplifted life.

An uplifted point of view means that you see

beneath the ordinary difficulties of things,

and you're able to make contact with

the divine Wise Mind."

Part Two

What Your Wise Mind Might Tell You

Chapter Thirteen

What Your Wise Mind Might Tell You

Removing the veil that clouds the view of our God Presence is seeing and feeling through our open hearts. When our hearts are open, we know that all is love, that we are whole and complete. . . .

—Arnold Patent, The Journey

Opening the Wise Mind Pages

In addition to the Wise Mind Process, you'll find here some ancient and current truths that are the province of the Wise Mind. They are the stuff that the Wise Mind is made of. If at all possible, see if you can read these truths with a "beginner's mind," even if you're already advanced on your path.

As you allow your consciousness to penetrate each page, you may find yourself reaching levels of understanding that are deeper than you've known before. This time you may be able to truly comprehend something that you'd previously known conceptually. Your experience of reading this book can be dynamic and interactive, and it can take you deeply into your own self-knowledge.

If you don't agree with something in the following pages, that's fine. See what your own Wise Mind wants to tell you. That's the whole idea anyway, to come to your own understanding of what's real. The following pages may be a springboard for the development and refinement of your own vantage point.

The purpose is to open your understanding, take off the blinders, and be attuned to the depth and brilliance of your Wise Mind.

Do Not Drive with Your Sunshades On

One day I went to the Toyota dealer, and I bought some sunshades for my car. I read the directions, which said, "Do not drive with the sunshades on." When I imagined myself driving with those opaque silver sunshades attached to the windshield of my car, I found the image hilarious. I laughed about it every time I entered my car. And because I was paying so much attention to it, I wondered, "What could this possibly be saying to me?" Then in one flash of a moment, I got it. My Wise Mind told me that as I'm living my life, I need to take the blinders off. I need to navigate my life or drive the vehicle within myself without my blinders on. Wake up. Open up. That was the message to me.

Advanced Ways of Living

There are advanced ways of living in this world. Enlightened masters see light and love permeating everything. They understand that everything is an emanation from a higher plane. Everything is made of the stuff of higher consciousness, and if you can see this with your own eyes, you can lead an uplifted life. An uplifted point of view means that you see beneath the ordinary difficulties of things, and you're able to make contact with the divine Wise Mind. We came to this earth to know the love and wisdom of the universe. That is what can lift us up beyond the perceived challenges of our lives.

The spiritual teacher Grady Clair Porter has said:

> I consistently allow myself to feel the Love of the Universe that showers upon me and all else in this beautiful, infinite day. . . . I feel, with unconditional trust, that I am the whole of the Universe; all that I see is Me. . . . I feel the warmth and peace of unconditionally loving my own infinite Self. [vi]

What Your Wise Mind Might Tell You

What follows in the next chapters are truths of the Universe that are the province of the Wise Mind. Fully being with them provides opportunities for profound transformation of all the challenging circumstances of our lives. In the seventies, there was a perfect word for this from the book *Stranger in a Strange Land*. The word is *grok*, and it means that you see deeply into something, understanding it experientially from the inside out, often in a flash of a moment. So, even if you "know" something written about in the following pages, let yourself grok it, and it will be certain to create huge transformational shifts in your universe and in your understanding.

Chapter Fourteen

What Your Wise Mind Might Tell You

#1

Everything in your life is an opportunity for transformation.

See the advantage in everything.
This can help you to have a happy life
No matter what the obstacles may seem to be.

—The Inner Guide, SamuEl,
Healing Is Remembering Who You Are, by Marilyn Gordon

Years ago I created an experience of initiation for myself, one in which I was learning mastery and the knowing of my Self. It took place in a rainy fall season in the early 1970s, and for a short while I had been living in a small tent in the tiny coastal town of Bolinas, California. I was growing more and more uncomfortable every day. I had just ended a relationship, and I hadn't created the next place to live yet, so I set up a tent, put a rug on the makeshift floor, brought some books, a light, and some paper to write on, and I prayed with great fervor. And yes, it was beginning to rain. Sometimes I was buoyed up by courage; at other times I was terrified. In my mind the proverbial creatures of the dark could come and get me, or so I sometimes thought, or I could get rain-soaked from the impending rainy season or infested with sow bugs—or so it seemed. I alternately felt myself to be a victim and then a pioneer standing at the edge of something very new. All of this was my perception.

I went soon to a fair in a nearby town, and a wandering poet-minstrel came up to me with a strangely knowing smile on his face. He said to me, "I have a poem for you." He inched close to my ear, and he whispered this haiku poem:

> Since my house burned down,
> Now I have a better view of the rising moon.

I nearly fell over. I had been living with the entire natural world, and the opportunity to expand into it was huge, but I'd been looking at the walls of my tent and not at the infinite space of the great limitless world. There was so much I wasn't seeing. I wasn't seeing the opportunity to expand my awareness, to be with the natural world and the great moment in time that was there for me to grow. This experience was serving a larger purpose for me. I was learning detachment and faith. I was learning to be in the moment and not worry if I'd ever have a home again. In that instant I dropped all feelings of victimization, and I knew that I was in another state of consciousness. The synchronicity of the wandering poet's act of reciting that poem to me was astonishing; I was in an altered state of mind. This is an experience of the Wise Mind externalized, and it was a transformational experience that shifted my consciousness and my life. This was a turning-point moment for me. I had set up this situation for myself to shift my awareness, and when I accomplished that, I had no need to stay in my tent any longer, and I moved on.

The Ultimate Obstacle Course

Knowing wisdom and love is ultimately the reason why we came to this Earth. Every experience we have offers us the opportunity to enter an expanded state of consciousness, and the more we enter, the more self-realized we become. So, as in myths of heroes and heroines, we create obstacles to overcome so that we can ultimately find our true power. Myths of such perceived obstacle courses are everywhere: Dorothy wants to get back home from Oz; Alice seeks to return to her bed and her cat; Parsifal the knight searches for the Holy Grail; Gulliver, Ulysses, and Odysseus search for their freedom.

Everyone creates something to prevail over—a difficult relationship, a health issue, fears, cruelties, self-doubt, or grief. In myths these have been symbolized as enchanted forests, turbulent seas, monster worlds, or violent battlefields. Once you reframe your issues as the scenario for your self-realization instead of an agonizing burden, you shift the nature of your reality. In all perceived difficulties and challenges, souls are learning something that advances them on their paths.

The Wise Mind Puts It in Perspective

The moment you stand back and allow your Wise Mind to assist you in seeing the more panoramic view of what's taking place in your experience, the more you're able to handle it and ultimately move to another level of it. "What would my Wise Mind tell me about this?" is the transformational question we can always ask. When you ask this question, you find spiritual gifts of deep wisdom that show you the significance of all the experiences you've created in your life.

We create events and experiences in patterns. We repeat situations in one form or another until we get the understanding. When we see that we are repeating something over and over, we can ask the Wise Mind, "How have I created this in my life? What am I learning from this?" We create events and circumstances in our lives so that we can have a human experience and can ultimately learn mastery. We, as the Soul Self, may have created something even before we were born. The purpose is to give us the experience of being human so that from the human state, we can then create mastery. Everything, then, is an opportunity for self-knowledge and wisdom. Seeing everything as loving and supportive, and allowing ourselves to be joyful no matter what the circumstance, is always an option. If we're willing to see everything from the mountaintop, we can see through everyone and everything into the heart and soul of All That Is.

Chapter Fifteen

What Your Wise Mind Might Tell You
#2
It's possible to wake up from the illusion of darkness at any moment.

It is your birthright to know the infinite love that is within you,
and when you experience it, you can walk with love
amidst all the experiences of the world.

—The Inner Guide, SamuEl,
Healing Is Remembering Who You Are, by Marilyn Gordon

You have the ability to shift your thoughts and life, to transform the illusion of darkness into the reality of light. When you're ready to see something in your life in a new way, your consciousness can shift as if by a miracle. You may have been preparing for this instant for a long time, and then when you're ready, you're able to create a new version of your life. When the power of transformation enters your consciousness, it can heal your childhood, your relationships, your emotions your work, your body— your life.

I AM the Power of Healing

Many years ago in the seventies, I was experiencing some particularly distressing emotional upheaval. It was triggered by a sudden loss that was not major, but it grew into a much larger experience. For several months I felt worthless and I grieved. I'd cry at nothing. Someone told me that I was going through an opening of all my "centers," but it certainly didn't feel that way. One day I experienced an "I've had it" moment, and I knew that this was the instant that I'd make a significant internal shift in this state of mind that had been limiting my life.

I'd been reading a book that I bought in the town of Mt. Shasta, a small beautiful town at the foot of the majestic mountain. There was a tiny store in the town called the I AM Society with a quaint reading room and intriguing posters and books. I bought a hardbound green book called *The I AM Discourses*. Its language was dynamic and euphoric—all about the great transcendent magnetic beams of magnificent universal power that were available to us when we invoke them. The key words were I AM. Saying these words could cause the heavens to open and the beams to flow radiantly from the ultimate Source of electromagnetic power.

As I read this small green volume, I knew that this power could heal the difficulties of life and that my emotional upheaval could come to an end. On the inner level, I was given an invocation: "I AM the power of healing, and I AM healing myself now." I made an agreement with myself to say it as often as I possibly could, especially when darkness of the mind would come forth. I realized that it was more than an affirmation. Each time I said it, I was reaching to the Divine, to the healing powers of the Universe. In this way I was determined to be free from the debilitating state of consciousness I was creating from within myself. I had paid a great deal of attention to my difficult thought process prior to this—looked at the dynamics from many angles, including past lives, childhood, life traumas, and more. Yet the pattern had persisted.

When I began to say, "I AM the power of healing, and I AM healing myself now," I knew I was drawing upon the great universal power. I imagined it as beams from the Universe shining upon me, illuminating me. I also felt those beams coming from within myself. If thoughts would bubble up from the subterranean inner mind, the ocean of thought forms, I would counter them with my refrain. "No, I AM the power of healing. No, these thoughts have no power over me." So thoughts of not being good enough or of any other insufficiency or darkness no longer held dominion. I remembered my agreement with myself that told me to persevere, to not allow darkness to take hold. I said no to it—to the anonymous voices within myself.

As I continued to proclaim my true nature, I experienced strength, and I became centered and clear. Within two days I was utterly transformed. I could close my eyes and experience beams of light entering the top of my head and moving through my body, and I could feel the beams of light radiating from my own heart.

The Wise Mind and the Healing Power

Years later I could add more to this: the Wise Mind Process. I could come to know and describe the difficult thoughts and experiences, I could breathe into them, I could ask my Wise Mind about them, imagine myself as I'd like to be, and then I could say my powerful words of invocation to the healing power. All I had to do was remember.

Most of the time I see the healing power as beams of light. Others have experienced it as a great ocean or a triumphant mountain, a voice, an angel, a great forest sunlight, or a divine experience of love. This representation is very personal. However it shows its face, its presence is magnificent, and it allows us to wake up from the darkness.

Transformation in a Moment

Transformation itself doesn't need to take any time. It can be instantaneous, a great "Aha!" moment in which you see things clearly with your Wise Mind, and you make a substantive shift. The possibility is inspiring, and it happens at exactly the right time.

Manifestation Power

In the same way that the universal power fuels the healing process, it also works as a catalyst for manifestation. Through this connection with the ultimate power, we can create substantive shifts in any area of life. We can create greater prosperity, shift health concerns, and transform relationships. The Wise Mind leads the way in both manifestation and healing power. It shows us where to look, assists us in identifying and releasing any obstacles along the way, and sends forth powerful energies to take us to higher levels of life.

Chapter Sixteen

What Your Wise Mind Might Tell You
#3
Your perspective is what matters.

Overheard:
"Are you wearing that hat because it's a bad hair day?"
"No, I'm wearing it because it's a good hat day!"

No matter what events are taking place in your life, it's how you perceive them that matters. Some souls have created time in jails and concentration camps, and they've used this time to advance their soul's progress. They've been able to contemplate the meaning of existence even in these challenging circumstances, and they've realized that they can lift up their consciousness even in the midst of challenging circumstances. If we could only stand back and see the panoramic perspective, we might be very surprised at what we'd understand: that the true energy of the universe is love, and if we see from an advanced perspective, we can lift ourselves higher and higher.

Take your immediate family, for example. Standing back from them, you can understand that they're not what you thought them to be. You can see that all others in your life are beings who are reflecting where you are. When you feel the love in everyone, your perception of them shifts. In standing back and shifting your perspective, great transformation can take place. *A Course in Miracles* says, "I am determined to see things differently." When you do, you see what seems to be the behavior of others as a reflection of your self.

One woman had experienced sexual abuse by her father. She cried and moved through her sadness and anger, and she was able to release those deep feelings. Then she had an epiphany. She realized that her mind had been holding on to the image of a perpetrator and keeping herself stuck that way. She let that dissolve as she stood back and viewed her life. From this great overview, her Wise Mind told her that this had been a profound learning experience. She was able to get to another level of understanding in which she was empowered enough to release and heal. There are opportunities to see that love is the true energy of the universe, and the illusion of darkness then turns into light.

Another woman said, "When I was fourteen years old, I couldn't understand why I couldn't have my mother's love. I felt a burning in my chest, and every night I would meditate in my bed. At some time in this process, my Wise Mind showed me my mother's entire lineage. I saw her life and the lives that made her, and I had great compassion for her. I saw my mother completely differently after that."

When you shift your perspective enough, you can ultimately have compassion for everyone. If you can expand your perspective, you can see that all the stories are just that—stories—and there is another level of truth.

Witness Consciousness

Witness consciousness is a profound state for healing and transformation. It is the ability to step out of the "pea soup" of your experience and to see it from a greatly expanded point of view. It can be called "cosmic vision" or "standing back," and it is a part of the Wise Mind. Whatever you wish to call it, it is a powerful state.

Standing back gives you perspective, and it helps you to see a situation with a different focus. It's like putting up a picture on the wall. It's hard to see if it's straight when you stand very close, but when you move away, you can see exactly how to position it.

The book *A Course in Miracles* points out that we don't really see things the way they are. There is another way to see everything. Enlightened masters understand that everything is consciousness. These masters see only light and beauty, and they understand that there is an advanced way of being in this world. We interpret our lives through the lens of our consciousness. It's possible to see with a transformed perspective with the assistance of the Wise Mind.

Chapter Seventeen

What Your Wise Mind Might Tell You
#4
You create thought and feeling patterns that determine your reality.

The thoughts you hold are mighty, and illusions are
as strong in their effects as is the truth. . . .
The world is nothing in itself.
Your mind must give it meaning.
There is no world apart from your wish,
and herein lies your ultimate release.
Change your mind on what you want to see,
and all the world must change accordingly.
"'I loose the world from all I thought it was."

—*A Course in Miracles, Lesson 132*

We create thought and feeling patterns in our consciousness. And we play these habitual tendencies of mind and emotion like endless tape loops or tendencies of mind that create suffering or joy. We create all kinds of patterns in our minds.

One woman heard the bouncing sounds of a neighbor's basketball. She had an anxiety attack. Another woman heard waves "slapping up" against rocks. She couldn't sleep all night long. Both of these women had internal memories of the sounds and emotions of family abuse, and both of them gave significance to the patterns that could become stimulated by similar external events.

We all create patterns of mind and feelings so that we can solidify the experience of being human. We do this so that we can ultimately become free by creating mastery. We can become free from these patterns by first becoming aware of what they are. The Wise Mind Process will help us to do this, and then we can release and transform the patterns so that we can live on more expanded levels of life.

There are thought and feeling patterns that sound like: "I'm no good. Oh, my God, I'm so short or fat or tall. I'm going to fail that test, I'm going to ruin this marriage, I always get mistreated, I'll never make it." These and other habitual thoughts and feelings are powerful ways to reinforce the state of being human, and they also present opportunities to move to another level of living once they're overcome. We can transform these patterns or tape loops. They exist at the level of the subconscious mind, the deep inner mind, and we can pay attention to them by describing them, breathing into them and breaking them up into tiny molecules, asking our Wise Mind to tell us about them, imagining ourselves as we'd like to be, and anchoring the transformation. In this case we take a leap into a different level of consciousness where we can shift the forms and transform our lives.

The Wise Mind and Thought and Feeling Patterns

Your Wise Mind's innate wisdom tells you what you need to know to shift your thinking. One woman weighed three hundred pounds. She had lost forty, but she was still in a state of self-doubt. So she asked her Wise Mind to show her something about this. Her Wise Mind took her on a trip in an airplane. She said it was the most joyful ride she'd ever had. Her Wise Mind then said to her, "Sit back and let the pilot fly the plane." Her Wise Mind continued, "You need to feel more connection with others, let Spirit guide your life, and feel lighter in Spirit." Before she heard her Wise Mind tell her to "lighten up," her old patterns of thought and feeling had reinforced her self-doubt, told her she could never be the way she wanted to be. She now knew that by connecting with the true "Pilot of the Universe," she could let her life soar.

Chapter Eighteen

What Your Wise Mind Might Tell You
#5
You're the way you are, not the way you were.

You can say to yourself,
"I'm creating this.
It's not real.
It's completely made up.
It's a creation of my Consciousness.
I reclaim power from this creation now."

—Robert Scheinfeld, *Busting Loose from the Money Game*

Whatever you focus on expands, so it's a good idea to focus on the happiness and love that are innate to every person rather than dwelling on the perceived wounds and misfortunes that are the creations of people's minds. It's helpful to pay attention to the perceived pain, but dwelling on it keeps the negativity alive and gives it credence. Concentrating on happiness and love reminds you of what's innately at the core of all things and gives you fuel for true transformation.

Jody wanted to transform the way she reacted with fear and anger to everyday things. This habit of mind baffled her, as she had a great life—with work and a relationship she loved. She had several choices. She could go back to the places of perceived pain and refuel them, or she could accentuate the happiness and joy and open herself to resonating more and more with it. In a second, she knew she wanted to choose joy.

She didn't bypass the difficult emotions. She paid attention to them, as she described them in as much detail as she could. Then she released these feelings, and she allowed her Wise Mind to talk to her. It said to her:

> Don't grasp onto the fear. Allow it to flow. Keep breathing. Allow yourself to feel calm, relaxed, and peaceful. Let the word serenity reverberate through you. Then you'll feel more connected to your true self, and then you'll be free of the old emotions.

So first she paid attention, but she didn't dwell on the challenges. She moved her consciousness to another level so that the door to serenity and love could open.

The Difficulties of the Past Are Over

It's possible to clear the memories from your mind and cells. More than likely, what happened before is not happening anymore. You may say, "I've always done it that way. It's my hurt inner child that's operating now, and that's why I'm being sensitive." Or you might say, "I've always eaten that, so that's what I do now." Or, "I've always responded to my father or my mother that way, and that's the way I do it now."

The truth is that every moment, the molecules of your being shift as your consciousness expands. You're not that old self anymore. Ellen felt she ate too much. She realized that as she was growing up, there was "never enough." She also knew that now she was living in a state of abundance, and there was certainly enough. Her Wise Mind told her to imagine the old part of herself and heal her, to shine the light of abundance and enlightenment on her. This brought Ellen into the present, in which she realized that she wasn't this girl any longer and that she could now bring all parts of herself into a new state of consciousness. She was able to curb her need to overeat and hoard her food and to begin to live right now.

The same healing possibilities exist for adult children whose parents and grandparents were in concentration camps or suffered the Depression years, or for people who believe they starved to death in other incarnations. When they realize that they're here now, they can shift these deeply ingrained patterns. Consider that these patterns and thoughts have no reality now, and then consider the power that exists in that understanding.

There is always an opportunity for transformation. You're not the same person you thought you were. You're a divine being, and your Wise Mind will eternally be present to assist you in remembering that.

Transforming the Frozen Pictures in the Soul

I call these old patterns "Frozen Pictures in the Soul." These are freeze-framed inner pictures, stories we've told ourselves and illusions we've subscribed to that we seem to have frozen within ourselves. They live within a magnificent imaginary database of the deep inner mind, like statues from that childhood game in which someone yells "Freeze!" and you stand suspended in a posture, frozen in time. Here you'll find made-up images of the hungry baby self, the lonely teenager, the rejected lover— as well as the happy children and joyous adults who are freeze-framed as well.

We've created these pictures inside ourselves, and it can be a life-transforming event to locate them inside. When we pay attention to them for a short while, great shifts can take place. It's as if they've gone to sleep in an uncomfortable position, and they've been asleep for so long that now they need some assistance in waking up. We put them to sleep, and we can wake them up and transform them. Many of our myths give expression to this, including Rip Van Winkle and Sleeping Beauty. Our wax museums and galleries are filled with casts of characters frozen in a moment in time.

Once retrieved and paid attention to briefly, all the perceived beings inside can be awakened, loved, and transformed. Then you can understand that they're not even real, and you can awaken to an expanded reality. You wake up from the dream of insufficiency, neglect, fear, and lack of love. This is the beginning of the process of true transformation.

The Wise Mind Comes to the Rescue

The first step, then, is to pay attention briefly to what you find. Just explore it and let yourself feel whatever it is you're feeling. Find out whatever you can about it. Ask it as many questions as you like. "Who are you? What's happening? What do I need to know?" Then you breathe into it and exhale it out. And then you ask your Wise Mind to tell you about this. It might tell you what the entire experience has meant to your growth. It may want to offer you a transformed way of looking at the entire experience. And then who you'd like to be can keep on expanding so that you can live in a wonderful new way.

You Can Live in Love and Joy Now

So now what was once the frozen picture exists in a transformed state, and this gives you the possibilities of being here in this very moment. You can breathe freely, knowing that a perceived part of you has been released into love and joy. This freedom in the soul is actually a state of grace, and it comes through a process of connection with your Wise Mind and the process of transformation. It comes with that wake-up touch that expands your capacity to experience happiness and love.

Chapter Nineteen

What Your Wise Mind Might Tell You
#6
Perceived wounds can pierce you open.

There is a perfection to everything, a beauty in everything.
In what you see as difficult times, the perfection may be hard to see, but
any moment the meaning of everything can open up before you.

—The Inner Guide, SamuEl,
Healing Is Remembering Who You Are, by Marilyn Gordon

All the perceived hurts and wounds in your awareness can give you an opportunity for opening up and can allow you to see beauty or love—or they can reinforce a more negative reality. Every intense reality can be a loving opportunity for you to move higher and higher in your consciousness. Some people need to be shocked awake from the sleep of their existences. Others can get the message in more subtle ways.

Some have called pain a teacher or a friend, as the perceived painful events have often led to transcendent experiences. The perceived wounds can lead to profound transformation and the opening of your eyes.

The Power of the Wounded Healer

One important way of understanding illness or difficulty is to see these states as processes by which an individual becomes transformed and is then able to assist others. Called the "wounded healer" paradigm, it is for many a process of initiation and of connection to a more expanded way of life. Of course, not everyone who enters difficult times becomes awakened by them. But for some who do, it is a process of metamorphosis. And even if the difficulty is not truly real in the most expanded sense of the word, the perception of difficulty can become an opportunity for true liberation, as we overturn rocks and boulders in consciousness and set free joy and love.

You may have your own experience with this. Your Soul Self may create something very difficult in your experience. Perhaps it is a great physical or psychological illness or an addiction or a loss. You may even be called to the brink of death. And then your Wise Mind might speak to you, telling you of the possibility of moving into another level of your life. When you move to another level of yourself, your life changes. Your personality and interests change. You may be led to work with others to help uplift and heal them. You cannot go back to the life you once led. You are operating on an entirely new plane of existence.

New Ways of Being

This is the transformation of the wounded healer. It's a process of becoming initiated and transformed, in which you lift yourself into epiphanies of insight and new ways of being. Healers and shamans, for example, have awakened from their own personal illusions of darkness. Sometimes they experience dire illnesses in which they are on the brink of death, they hear an inner voice telling them that a new life is on the horizon, they understand their particular predicament, and then they awaken to a new life.

You can ask, "What would my Wise Mind like to tell me about this situation?" And you can then channel your own wisdom to find ways to awaken. Through the wounded healer paradigm, you can come to know that whatever is taking place is an opportunity for transformation. You understand that the greatest difficulty may be the springboard for ultimate illumination. This kind of understanding goes beyond the idea of controlling habits or getting rid of symptoms. This way of seeing knows that healing is a process in which consciousness is being awakened. We move beyond the difficulties into higher and higher states of wisdom and love.

By paying attention to our experiences, learning the ways of releasing them, and understanding the art of spiritual transformation, we can lift up all experiences of woundedness and enter the realms of light.

Chapter Twenty

What Your Wise Mind Might Tell You
#7
Inner resistances can be recognized and transformed.

Blessed are the men and women
who are planted in your earth, in your garden,
who transform their darkness to light
—The Odes of Solomon,
The Enlightened Heart, ed. Stephen Mitchell

Many people resist transformation. We keep ourselves in comfort zones through our resistances, zones that may not truly be comfortable but are so familiar that they seem to be resting places. We may hold onto the illusions of depression and fear because we know them well. Or we keep an outworn relationship because we're used to it. We created it in our consciousness, and we hold onto it for dear life. But what would it be like to feel the new levels of joy that waiting for us inside our soul?

We may have resistances to the transformed state because we find it hard to move from our experiences of comfort. Sometimes it's hard to fathom how to live in greatness, to experience the "great Self." What would it be like to be Self-realized? What would it be like to manifest? What would it be like to do what you came here to do? What would it be like to make wise choices and become free?

Where Do Resistances Come From?

We create our own resistances so that we can learn from them. We are powerful creators, and when we recognize that we've been hiding under these limitations, we can create new and expanded ways of being. We can look for ways to break free. And here's where the Wise Mind comes in.

A Deeper Look

Beth worked a nine-to-five job; the bosses wanted more and more overtime, and she was beginning to get tired. More than this, she had dreams for her life. She'd invented some gadgets she dreamed of bringing to the marketplace, some products for business and for pets, but she had created layer upon layer of life experiences that limited any action on her part. She told herself she had too many papers and too many extraneous projects in her office. She needed to clean it, but she never did. She also told herself she didn't know enough about how to go about her business.

Her Wise Mind told her,

> You've been thinking you're not good enough. You've been thinking that you're keeping yourself safe by limiting yourself. But now you can do something else. You can thank the force of limitation that you've created, and now you can move on.

Beth decided to do the entire Wise Mind Process. She first paid attention to the force of limitation that she felt inside; she listened to it and felt it in her body. She looked at what she might have been trying to accomplish through limitation all these years and how she had created it in her consciousness.

She breathed into it, and she breathed it out.

Her Wise Mind told her more:

> You can now appreciate—and even love—this limiting force, and through your love and appreciation for its having worked to keep you safe and allowed you to be a human being, you might extricate yourself from it in a gentle and even beautiful way. You can now see and feel love and happiness, and you can create whatever new life you'd like.

She then imagined the success of her ventures, and she saw herself as empowered and free to realize her dream. Her healing phrase was "great success."

When you understand your creation of these limiting forces, you can create powerful shifts. This way you can go beyond limitations, and you can live your life in entirely new ways.

Loving the Resistance

We've already talked about the yogi Milarepa, who gave up swatting at his perceived demons when one of them wouldn't leave. To that one particularly persevering one, he finally said, "Okay. Come and sit down and have some tea with me, and we'll talk about the teachings." This so startled the demon that it immediately left! This is the very nature of acceptance. Through it, transformation comes.

Rumi in his "Guest House" poem counsels us to honorably treat the sorrows, shame, and negative thoughts and invite them in as guests, seeing that we may have created each one as a "guide from beyond." This is not to say that you ask any of them to take up residence in your guest house forever. You simply pay attention and then transform them. You can invite in the forces of "Nobody loves me" or "I'm completely alone" or "I'm terrified of that." When these forces sit down at the table with you, they are shifted just by your state of mind. They haven't been expecting such a welcome. They're used to being ignored or pushed down or even having their influence serve without any boundaries. You can give love to sadness, regret, and even anger, which is like kissing the proverbial frog and turning it into a prince. They are transmuted through the power of awareness and love.

Resistances as Human

The Wise Mind knows that resistances are not, in and of themselves, bad. The experience of limitation is a part of the experience of being human. And yet there is a greater way to live—with your light and wisdom shining. You can recognize the limitation but not wallow in it. You then take the next step, and when you do take it, it is the step that transforms your life.

Beyond the Status Quo

There are always so many reasons for keeping the status quo. Often there are perceived secondary gains ("If I keep this weight, no men will bother me"). Or fears ("If I get a new job, I might fail to do well"). Or conditioned considerations ("If I do that, I'll be better than my mother or father or brother, and that's not okay"). These are all just your beliefs and thoughts.

You have to want to go beyond these considerations more than you want to hold onto them. Everything in life is an opportunity for awakening to our greatness and our strength. Working with the limitations is a part of the powerful work of transformation, and the Wise Mind is here as a dedicated guide in this magnificent process of moving from the illusion of darkness into the reality of light.

Chapter Twenty-One

What Your Wise Mind Might Tell You
#8
You can become the nonjudgmental witness of your life and thoughts.

*In standing back
from your own mind
you begin to understand all things.*

—Lao Tzu, Tao Te Ching

We've already talked about Lao Tzu's lines in his book of poetic verses, the Tao Te Ching. In talking of "standing back from your own mind," he is elucidating the great secret of witness consciousness, the ability to see your life from another state of consciousness. This is a high healing state. It's the ability to step out of the mire of the experience and to see it from a greatly expanded point of view, from the skybox or the high joy vibration.

Witness consciousness is a state of meditation. You're observing yourself as an actor in—or as the director of—the play. When you expand awareness this way, you're in touch with a high level of truth. You have the ability to witness, to observe without judgment. From this vantage point, clarity comes, and it may reveal deep truths, the truths of the Wise Mind.

The Witness Doesn't Judge

The biggest problem comes in when we stand back and judge ourselves harshly. When that happens, you can be certain it's not a Wise Mind witness state. It's from ego, a critical judgmental ego state. The Wise Mind is a nonjudgmental witness. Its job is to see the overview, to see from an expanded state of understanding, and then to support, love, and heal. It shows us the cosmic overview of the vast panorama of experience. When you move your consciousness into higher states, you expand into love and wisdom. You see your life in new ways. You can see the world in new ways as well—that there is a force of love behind everything, even if it may not seem so at the moment, and that we can create this in our consciousness through our own creative power.

Standing Back

The capacity to stand back and see the panorama of events of your life on the screen of awareness is a high healing state. A very accomplished woman, a physician named Ann, had a childhood in which she'd felt much abandonment and sadness. By consistently becoming the witness and paying careful attention to the abandoned girl she created to exist within herself, she was able to love every part of herself. She had created in her consciousness the pain of perceived abandonment and the fear that she'd live in that darkness forever. When the love arose in her, she felt it arise from a deep source, and through her Wise Mind she instantly understood that this was part of her human experience. She understood that her patients also had the same life creations, and she was able to assist them because her heart was open. She was now able to return to the enlightened, compassionate Self that was her essence.

When we can love everything that had once seemed difficult, we can feel a sense of empowerment. Everything is by its very nature infused with light. That is its highest truth, and we are invited to expand our ability to see it. The development of a transformed consciousness is one of the greatest gifts of our existence.

Chapter Twenty-Two

What Your Wise Mind Might Tell You
#9
The true root cause of all your issues is separation from the Infinite Source.

I AM not my body, not my mind. Immortal Self I AM.

—*Yoga Prayer*

To be connected to the universal energy, the great healing power, is to be in touch with the transcendent, radiant power of the universe. Some people experience it visually. Others perceive it on the level of feeling or as a kinesthetic phenomenon. You might experience it as a ray that pours down into you, perhaps through the top of your head and down into your entire body and mind. You might know it as an emanation of light that radiates from you, especially from your heart. It may appear to you in symbolic form, as an ocean or a radiant sun. It may be on a mental level, a thought that a force in the universe is the substratum of all that is and that comprises every single cell in your being and everything else as well.

You may attune to this great power through an advanced being, such as Jesus or Moses or Krishna or

Quan Yin. You may know it as love itself. It may come to you as the Wise Mind, an abiding wisdom that sees through and knows all things.

And yet there are those times when this radiant Presence seems to elude you. Where has it gone? The basic issue that every person is grappling with is the experience of separation, in which we feel negativities from being out of contact with the One.

Kashmir Shaivism, Again

In chapter 5 we talked about the beautifully intricate ancient teaching from the ninth century that explores the cosmology of how light can be temporarily obscured by darkness and how we can return to it again and again. Kashmir (because it's from Kashmir) Shaivism (about Shiva, a representation of God) is a brilliant philosophy. In the beginning was the perfect All-Oneness called Paramashiva (the Great One). And gradually, through our consciousness, everything began to devolve in our minds, instead of evolve, as if the light were covered by blinders or cloaks. Our job is to expand the contracted states and get back to Paramashiva, the Oneness, the love, wisdom, and greatness, again. Earlier we talked about how this process of concealing the light and then revealing it again as a process of awakening is the core of many great philosophies and cosmologies of the world.

The Remarkable Story of Alan

There was once a time when Alan was a happy, smiling, confident boy. Then when he was four, his mother died in childbirth. She had had thirteen children. Alan and two of his brothers were sent to an orphanage, and Alan perceived that the nuns there were very cruel. Alan needed to experience the infinite love. He knew about it in his mind, but he never felt it in his heart. Joy and light were still blocked. He expected that one day he'd open up, but it hadn't happened for him yet.

We did the Wise Mind Process. He first experienced that there was a curtain separating him from everyone else. There was tension in his body and a sense of inadequacy.

He then began to breathe into the experience, and as he breathed out, he broke it up into tiny molecules and dispersed it. The experience began to break up and disperse.

His Wise Mind told him:

> Live in the moment and let go. Make a real effort to give to others. You're putting these barriers over your own heart. You're opening now more and more, as the difficulties are over, done, complete, and you're ready now to open yourself to the experience of Oneness and love.

He then recalled what it had been like before his mother died: a feeling of expansiveness, openness, and light.

With these words and experiences came the opening of his heart and an abiding sense of peace and contentment. His special word to anchor in this experience was "give." He was now certainly on the path.

Reconnecting with the One

The moral of the story is that most of the difficulties we experience inside are due to a sense of separation from the One. Once we understand that, we can come back to the truth of our existence through the power of the higher self and the Wise Mind. In this way we remove the cloaks over our consciousness and return to true knowledge and love.

Chapter Twenty-Three

What Your Wise Mind Might Tell You
#10
You can uncover your true power.

Our power is our joy, abundance, peace, divinity, perfection, trust, gratitude, generosity, creativity, inspiration and unconditional love.

—Arnold Patent, The Journey

The Wise Mind lifts you out of old paradigms and is a true path of healing and ultimate enlightenment. Expanding the lens through which you view the universe takes you out of a self-limiting box and opens your consciousness and heart. You can move out the consciousness of suffering and pain, and you can experience the Universe as loving and supportive. You open into expanded levels, and you have the opportunity to understand how your life reflects your beliefs about it; you appreciate and accept your power; you understand that abundance is your ever-present natural state; you feel expansive and radiant love; and you experience yourself as the Power and Presence of God.

The Wise Mind Transforms Old Ways of Being

Joseph thought he was ugly. He did the Wise Mind process and found a profound darkness in his heart center. As he paid attention to it and watched it from within, the darkness began to move, to split open, and a light exploded from within him. He then felt the love for himself pouring through him, and he realized his own beauty as a fountain that comes from inside. His Wise Mind told him that he'd been identifying with an old version of himself that was conditioned by his life and his society. He pierced it open, and from this deep place, a great light of beauty emerged. He had come to this self-understanding from the highest and most sacred place within himself.

Just Imagine

Imagine yourself as powerful, loved and loving, and expansive. Imagine next how this understanding can transform the issues you've created in your life. Imagine your Wise Mind guiding you to a transformed existence. Imagine identifying with this expanded state of being, your true Self.

Chapter Twenty-Four

What Your Wise Mind Might Tell You
#11
You can understand that your inner experiences determine how you see the world.

In order to have our human experiences, we created the apparent reality that we are living outside the Oneness; that there are things and people that can affect us without our consent. The truth is that there is nothing outside of us; all that we see is our Self. This becomes our new reality when we open the belief in separation and accept the truth that we are the Power of God.

—Arnold Patent, *The Journey*

You may think that "forces out there" are having powerful effects on you, and that is a very powerful assumption. It's so powerful that often we create ourselves to be victims of these forces, and we blame them for whatever is taking place in our lives. This is not, however, the most powerful vantage point, and if seen from the highest state, it is certainly not the truest. At the very moment that we experience ourselves as creators rather than as receivers, empowerment is in place, and this is infinitely important in the process of transformation.

No "Forces Out There"

Linda's father had been abusive to the boiling point.

One day when she was a child, he threw hot water on her, and she was left with a huge wound. After she paid attention to her anger, fear, and her feeling of victimization, she knew that another step was possible. Linda saw, as she grew older and more powerful, that her own love could heal this picture in her mind. She knew that it had been a huge boulder in her consciousness and that underneath it was enlightenment and pure love. One day she rolled the boulder over, and the transformation came through her. Everything became illuminated with love, and she knew that the old thoughts were over. She realized that the incident she had created had led her onward to higher and higher levels of understanding.

Moving Out of the Web of Low Self-Worth

Another woman named Judith was intelligent and skilled in her work as a counselor, yet she had a nagging feeling of being a failure. She did the Wise Mind Process, and she made some life-transforming discoveries. As Judith looked inside herself, she saw an image of her father that she had created in her consciousness. In this picture he looked scared and tense with a furrowed brow. She saw that he was yearning for something. Deep down, he didn't love himself. She breathed into this and then dispersed it on the exhalation. Her Wise Mind then spoke to her:

> Give love to yourself, and realize that you have more power and worth than you ever imagined.

Her healing words were, "I am the source of love." This experience was a catalyst for Judith to continue her work, give herself love and approval, and allow herself to succeed.

How a Woman Transformed Her Relationship

Karen had been married for over a year now. She was in her fifties, and John was twenty years older. Their relationship was very loving, but one thing bothered Karen profoundly. He'd be negative behind the wheel of his car and negative in the ways he often spoke about life. He always acted lovingly toward Karen, though she got angry at his negativity and she wanted to be less aggravated about it. She decided to do the Wise Mind Process.

Karen described the experience: "My heartbeat is very rapid. I feel a huge sense of frustration and anger. My blood pressure feels like it's rising." She then took a deep breath into her experience and dispersed it. Her Wise Mind told her,

> Let him be, and be there for him. Be loving and caring instead of harsh and accusatory. Don't push him. If you just let him be, slowly he'll move in the right direction. If you allow him to be, he'll make a shift. Acknowledge him, have compassion for him, and show him another way. Realize that all you have to do is to shift your own awareness here, transform the negativity in your own self, and accept and love him.

Her healing phrase was "I accept and love." She knew that in truth, all she had to do was to transform her own awareness. She didn't need to shift anyone else. She was relieved and knew that now she was on a path toward harmony in her relationship. She felt that she was pointed in an upward direction. This made a great difference in her relationship with her husband. It all came from the expanded consciousness within her, brought to the forefront by the great Wise Mind. She never had any difficulty with this issue again.

Shirley Temple and Heidi

Here's a lighthearted, almost childlike, story with a profound message. Shirley Temple was a remarkable little girl. So was the main character she played in the movie Heidi. Heidi lived with her stepmother, who treated her as a nuisance and who wanted to give her away. Her stepmother finally took Heidi to live with her grandfather in a rustic alpine cabin. He was very rough-hewn and gruff, and he didn't speak to anyone. Instead of fretting and bemoaning her fate, Heidi would just smile at him and say, "Oh, Grandfather, can I get you some tea?" In a very short time her love helped his heart to open, as she didn't play into his negativities. She kept moving the vibration higher and higher. She knew how to overcome the negativities of life. She didn't know this, but she naturally was able to elevate her consciousness to understand that everything that's taking place is a choice in consciousness. She knew how to transform the pictures of reality and move her life into higher and higher levels.

There's No THERE There

If you have old pictures your mind of being the victim of someone else's actions, take another look, and travel to the core of love in everything in the universe. Let the picture melt away, and come back to the love. This is how you can have a happy mind and happy life, and you can go beyond all you thought was real—into the true reality of ultimate wisdom and love.

Chapter Twenty-Five

What Your Wise Mind Might Tell You
#12
You can experience deep peace.

*Out beyond ideas of wrongdoing and rightdoing
there is a field. I'll meet you there.*

*When the soul lies down in that grass,
The world is too full to talk about.*

—Rumi, trans. Coleman Barks

As I sit writing, I notice that my neighbor is hammering something into the wall. I'm somewhat amused at the synchronicity—as I'm writing about peace. And then I remember that the peace has nothing to do with the hammering. It's about my choice of whether or not to be annoyed by the noisy interlude or to go deeper within myself to the source of peace itself. Choosing the latter, I get down to the subject of experiencing deep peace and how it profoundly affects the process of healing.

It's about more than the landscape I saw last week—high up on a cliff looking out at the Pacific Ocean, as I watched the orange sun dissolve into the horizon. It's beyond even that. It goes right to the core of the self, the still point of the inner world, the place that is the beginning and end of all healing and transformation.

Inner peace and the Wise Mind are both qualities of the essence, the core of the Self. A woman named Sandra was dealing with a very difficult relationship. She did the Wise Mind Process, and she saw a very different scene. She felt strain going through her entire body and released some tears that she'd been holding in. She described herself as deeply sad, like thick, gray, and dismal storm clouds. She breathed into her experience and exhaled, and then her Wise Mind began to speak to her:

> Underneath your sadness is a landscape of you, a blanket of peace. There are rolling hills, carpets of green grass, breathtaking flowers, and you can come here to rest your soul anytime you like. Underneath your sadness, it's airy, light, and sunny. Come here at any time, and you'll transform all the troubles in your life.

Her healing phrase was "deep peace."

Sandra said that this was the most positive experience she'd ever had. By going to the central core of peace within, she found that her difficulties were no longer real. Here in this core, you can listen or feel or watch, and healing comes through. You're given the opportunity to be more peaceful about any of your issues—your finances, your health, your relationships, even the state of the world. The book *A Course in Miracles* says, "Peace is my most important priority." It also says, "I can see peace instead of this." And as one Zen monk wrote, "Over a cup of tea, I stopped the war."

A Place Where All the Wars Have Ended

In the essence of yourself, you can rest beside the still waters. Here the wars have ended, and there is stillness. Stillness itself can even be the answer you're looking for. When you're still, you stop the chattering of the restless mind, and you understand that just by being quiet, you've taken a leap into another level of your consciousness. The Bible says, "Peace, be still and know that I AM God."

What Your Wise Mind Might Tell You about Inner Peace

If you asked your Wise Mind about peace, it might say this to you:

> Peace is the greatest gift in the universe, more valuable than a lottery ticket, as it is pure gold itself. "I am the peace of God" is what you are inside. I AM showing you the way to happiness. Just be still for a moment. You are caught up in the letters of the alphabet, your thoughts. Just be quiet for a moment, and give yourself the opportunity to attune to the still voice of wisdom and love deep inside yourself. I have many gifts for you. I'm telling you that you're not who you think you are. You think you're someone limited, and yet you're boundless and eternal. This peace is a state of great transformation, and it's teaching you many things. Be in peace and silence, and you'll know the heart and soul of all things.

In this state of peace you can see more clearly, and you can see from the cosmic overview. Peace, wisdom, love, light, forgiveness—all of these will carry you across the Great Ocean. All of these qualities are woven from the same fabric as the Wise Mind, and all are qualities of the Infinite.

Chapter Twenty-Six

What Your Wise Mind Might Tell You
#13
You can shine light on anything in your life.

*There is no more worthy, more glorious or more potent work
than this work with light. If you really want to devote yourself
to something truly great and noble, this is it.*

—Omraam Mikhaël Aïvanhov, *Light Is a Living Spirit*

Soon after the tsunami brought its profound power to
the earth on December 26, 2004, I asked my Wise Mind
to tell me more about it. It said to me:

> The light is growing brighter on this planet, and from the
> higher levels, we see a transformation taking place. Many
> souls are moving to higher levels, even as they cross over to
> the other side. In this way, even though there is great travail
> on one level, there is an uplifting force at work, as we see it
> from a higher perspective.

The light is a powerful force for spiritual evolution, and
knowing it is our purpose on this earth. We are made of
light, and that light is divine in origin. The light heals,
comforts, illuminates, and transforms. There is light both
within and without. You can see it when you close your
eyes, and you can see it when you open them. When you
have contact with the light, you can shine it on everything
and everyone. The light transforms.

How You Can Experience More Light

If you close your eyes, you might see a pinpoint of light, or you may imagine an actual beam of light. You can allow this light to beam upon you. Now you may want to imagine that the light is beaming *from* you—from your heart, solar plexus, or the center of your forehead. You may imagine yourself surrounded in light, bathed in illuminating light rays. The light can be strong or gentle. It has profound healing power.

The light can transform any part of you. You can imagine the small child inside of you bathed in a blanket of light, healed and whole. Imagine your body bathed in light. Perceived pain can be infused with light rays. A relationship can be touched with the light and transformed. You can bathe the entire world in illuminating beams. You can send light to beings who've passed to the other side, understanding that they never actually die and that their souls live eternally.

You may experience the light as gold or white—or any other color that you feel is appropriate. Again, it may come from a beam that originates in the universe, or it may originate from within you. It may be warm, or it may have no temperature at all. See it, feel it, know it, and let the light shine. When we concentrate on it and let it shine, we come to know the luminous presence that is here for us at every moment.

Light . . . contains all the qualities and virtues of God . . . so concentrate your thought on light, rest in light, melt into light, soak yourself in light and picture the entire universe bathed in that light. Little by little as you do this, you will find that all the elements of your being begin to fall into place, that this light is bringing you true knowledge, lasting peace, inner balance and power. . . . Light is a living spirit.[vii]

The Light and the Wise Mind

Laura felt a lot of anxiety, and her current relationship was in shambles. She had many fears, and she knew she must heal herself now. She breathed into her fear. Her Wise Mind spoke to her:

> You're creating this all with your mind. You've been putting yourself in situations that aren't healthy for you. Imagine a big white swan going to a lighter level of existence. The light is here now, showing you what you need to do next, loving and healing you, transforming all your thoughts and feelings.

Her healing word, of course, was "light." This began the transformation of her relationship and her life. She, in fact, released the relationship and took the next step on her path.

Working with Beings of Light

Great Beings exist in realms of light, and they are forever in service to humanity to uplift, transform, and heal. Jesus, Moses, Buddha, Quan Yin, Mary, and Saint Germain are just a few of the advanced, illumined beings whose presence is always available to us whenever we ask. They are embodiments of the light that permeates the entire universe. To be able to bring more light to your body, your mind, and any situation is to set it in vibrational harmony with the healing power, the sacred energy of the universe.

Chapter Twenty-Seven

What Your Wise Mind Might Tell You
#14
Love fills you with transformational power.

My heart was split, and a flower appeared; and grace sprang up;
and it bore fruit for my God.
You split me, tore my heart open, filled me with love.
You poured your spirit into me
And you have made all things new; you have showed me
all things shining.
You have granted me perfect ease; I have become like Paradise,
a garden whose fruit is joy; and you are the sun upon me.

—*The Odes of Solomon, The Enlightened Heart, ed. Stephen Mitchell*

Love is the essential substance of the universe. It can be experienced as ecstasy, as deep caring, as a divine force field, and as a transcendent healing power. Molecules of love, in fact, are moving in every cell of our being. When you're not experiencing love, it's because you've created limitation. Whether you're experiencing it or not, the love is still always present. In addition to the perceived ills of the body, the absence of the experience of love is the greatest cause of the difficulties of human existence

How to Experience More Love

You can open your ability to experience love by healing your experience of separation, contacting your source of wisdom, and making a connection with the powerful force field in which love is all-pervading. You can also allow yourself to come to know what's standing in the way of experiencing love. By moving through and beyond the limitations, you will no doubt come into the essence, and that essence is made of love.

Anyone who has love carries the love vibration and can assist you in opening your own experience of love. Any great being who is unfettered with negativity can open you to love. Any friend or relative, past or present, alive or passed on, who has an open heart can heal the experience of separation in you, can open you up to knowing the expanded power of love.

You can also experience love independently of any external source. In your healing process, you can ask yourself, "Can I experience more love here?" And you can see what grace or miracles may help you to move beyond your limitations. Your Wise Mind will tell you where to find your resources.

As the poet Rumi says,

> Keep knocking, and the joy inside
> will eventually open a window and look to see
> who's there. [viii]

The Heart Changes Your Perspective

With your heart open, the difficulties of life are seen from an entirely new perspective. You are not the victim. There is a loving force that is propelling this world, even if at times it doesn't seem to be so. Love is there always, even if you're not aware of it at any given moment, even if there's no one else there to give or receive love.

The Wise Mind Speaks the Words of Love

Seeing a previously distressing situation with eyes of love can be extraordinarily healing. Janice had created food compulsions in her life. She binged frequently, and she also drank more than she knew was good for her. She went inside herself and did the Wise Mind Process. She experienced a gnawing feeling in her stomach. She breathed into it and exhaled. Her Wise Mind told her:

> You feel inside that you don't have enough food. Feel love for yourself, and know that you have plenty. You are becoming filled with love, and now you can feel a sense of fulfillment.

She felt so much love within herself, and being in touch with the love inside her helped her to let go of all alcohol, and she felt much more relaxed about food.

The Loving Power of Izumi

A number of years ago I visited my daughter, who was living in Japan. We had taken several trains and walked for miles to visit an *onzen*, a natural hot springs and inn that had traditional Japanese rooms with tatami mats on the floors and shoji screens for doors. My daughter had made a reservation at this particular inn in the town of Izu, and she didn't care for the place when we arrived. It was too noisy, she thought; you could hear the cars outside, and there was a schoolyard across the street and not a very beautiful view. The ceilings were too high, and it just wasn't comfortable here for her.

In the midst of these thoughts, a Japanese woman opened the shoji screens and entered our room. She had an extraordinarily wide and beautiful smile. She came in and said, "Hello! How wonderful to see you! I'm so happy that you're here." She had clean, black, shiny hair, a round, apple-cheeked face, and dancing eyes. You could feel the love streaming from her in the most natural and unpretentious way. Her name was Izumi, and she told us that she had lived in this place all her life. Her grandfather had built this historic inn to house the first Westerners who came to Japan on the Black Ships. He had built the ceilings high for them.

Then Izumi asked us, "Do you like to sing?" She had a karaoke machine there with the words on video, and I sang some Beatles songs in English—"Imagine" and "Yesterday"—and then Izumi and my daughter sang touchingly beautiful songs in Japanese. The room was filled with love. Who cared about a few car noises outside? This was Izumi's job, to welcome people with great love. She knew how to sweep away any clouds, to take the energy and lift it up. Izumi, with her heart full of love, came to pry open the doors of the heart one fine afternoon in the floating world of Japan.

Divine and Human Love

So, sometimes love comes in the form of other human beings, sometimes in the form of great advanced beings, and sometimes love is experienced independently of any human transmission, as a great radiant, dynamic blissful universal force. All of these forms of love are given as great gifts to us to uplift the difficulties of our lives.

Through the power of the Wise Mind, you can first experience and then send love to all parts of yourself that feel a sense of separation. You can touch with love the various inner parts of your human self that you've set up within you—the infant, the child, the teen, the critical, angry, abandoned, or alienated selves that are held within as still photos in the inner library of consciousness. You can transform archetypal parts of yourself, like the victim or critic. You can heal your mind and all the old thoughts you've had. You can touch these parts and experiences with great kindness, compassion, caring, and absolute divine love.

Healing the Deepest Places

You can hold all your old issues in the high-frequency vibration of love, and you can actually shift the way reality appears within you. William asked his Wise Mind to show him something about his feelings of loneliness. He found out that he was in an incubator for the first month of his life. Inside himself he chose to continue to experience a deep sense of coldness and alienation. With a stroke of healing power, he now brought his inner love to the situation. Within his own consciousness, he took the baby out of the incubator and held him. Then, with the loving power of his mind and heart, he surrounded this baby with the force of warm and flowing love. This transformed William to a new level of higher love energy, and his life opened to a new chapter.

Julie healed the baby inside herself also. Her Wise Mind told her to allow Christ to come to her. Jesus picked up the baby, told her how precious she was and how good it was that she was born, and gave her total love and protection. Great healing took place for her on a very deep level, as love came to heal all the deepest places of her soul.

Roger Craig, Love, and the NFL

I once had the great honor of flying to Oakland from Southern California with champion football player Roger Craig, and I didn't have any idea that he'd be a great spiritual teacher for me that day. I didn't know much about him, as I don't follow the game, but I learned that he was a magnanimous humanitarian. He acknowledged with love everyone who recognized him. He held their hands, patted their backs, struck up conversations with them, and showed them he was as happy to see them as they were him. Everyone he met at the airport and on the plane that day idolized him, and he idolized them back. In a word, he was a paragon of love. To meet everyone with love: that's what Roger Craig knew so well how to do. He knew the secret of love—to embrace everyone and everything from the deepest places in the heart.

The Quintessence of Love

A Course in Miracles speaks of this love:

> Put all your faith in the Love of God within you; eternal, changeless and forever unfailing. This is the answer to whatever confronts you today. Through the love of God within you, you can resolve all seeming difficulties without effort and in sure confidence.[ix]

Love is the basic energy of the universe, the energetic core within each molecule and cell in the world of matter. Love is the pinnacle and basic core of human experience, and it is ultimately what we came here on the earth to know.

Chapter Twenty-Eight

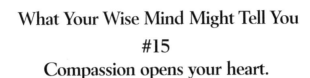

What Your Wise Mind Might Tell You
#15
Compassion opens your heart.

Choosing to recognize the unreality of the dream doesn't mean you shouldn't be sensitive to the needs and the feelings of people.

—Gary R. Renard, *The Disappearance of the Universe*

It's good to open your heart to the experiences of others. In truth, all others are projections of your own self. You can also open your heart to others who seem to create difficulty in your life. When you can open your heart to them, you're able to experience the form of love that is compassion.

Mother Teresa, in her compassion, assisted the indigent of Calcutta, loved them in what she called "their distressing disguise." Truly, everyone and everything is the universal life force in disguise.

Compassion for Yourself

Your Wise Mind might show you how to have compassion for your own self. You may have created negative thoughts and feelings about yourself inside. You may have done things you'd rather not have done. And yet you can find that core of love inside, which returns you to the pure understanding of your own divine nature. This compassion brings you back to the heart of wisdom, which reminds you that everything is as it needs to be. As you look at this with the power of your Wise Mind, you can see that the people around you, past and present, exist in you as you've created them. When you see the love at the core of all things, you allow your heart to open, and the compassion is free to express itself.

The Angry Neighbor, Compassion, and the Wise Mind

Judith had just moved into a new building, and she was very busy putting everything away and setting up her home. In her driveway there was space for four cars, and she knew that she could park in only one of those spaces. The first several days she was there, several of her visitors had made the mistake of parking in a neighbor's space. Judith tried to catch these incidents in time, but one of those days she didn't notice soon enough to tell them to move. As it had happened once before, the neighbor became livid. He rang the bell loudly and persistently to tell Judith about the mis-parked cars, and when Judith answered the door, the neighbor was exceedingly angry. As days passed, Judith couldn't let go of her own shock and anger at her neighbor's vitriol. Her Wise Mind said to her:

> Go to the core of this experience, and see your part in its creation. You can see in it whatever you choose to see. Let the anger go. This is an opportunity for you to shift into a higher level, as you release your own feelings and open to compassion in this situation.

This was yet another opportunity to move to another level of life. Her healing phrase was "release and heal." Her Wise Mind reminded her that this was a pattern that Judith came to this earth to resolve. It told her that her own reactive anger was from her own thoughts and feelings, and she had created the others in her life to behave in ways that would assist her to see the situations more clearly so that she could resolve and master them. Compassion and understanding did it for Judith, helped her to move out of habitual behavior patterns that held back her life.

There Is No "Other"

The spiritual truth here is that all "others" are really parts of our own selves as well as creations of our consciousness and mirrors of what's inside of us. It's not just that the characteristics of others are in us, but in the highest truth, we're all One. Our deep feelings of love and compassion can bring us back to the true transformation of life.

Chapter Twenty-Nine

What Your Wise Mind Might Tell You
#16
It's possible to forgive when you're ready.

Forgiveness is the willingness to open the energy locked
up in our judgments.
As we practice feeling forgiveness for a person whom we previously judged,
or are now judging, as being unloving toward us,
we loosen the attachment of the judgment to the feeling.
The universe is always helping us to clear all blocks to our
natural state of joyfulness.
It keeps offering us opportunities to forgive.

—Arnold Patent, *You Can Have It All*

Forgiveness is a state of consciousness that lifts you to the next level of yourself. In this next level everything is in divine order and all is as it needs to be. Only when you're ready is it time to forgive, to travel to the next levels. You may first need to process what's been happening and listen to what your Wise Mind might tell you about the situation. When you forgive, the burden you've been carrying is released, and you are finally able to experience spaciousness, light, pure air, and healing.

Wisdom That Makes Forgiveness Possible

True understanding, looking at the cosmic view of circumstances, compassion, and the readiness to forgive—all prepare the ground for the great release that forgiveness brings. *A Course in Miracles* says, "Forgiveness gives me everything I want." The *Course* is predicated on an understanding that the human self comes forth from the land of illusion, and therefore separation and negativity don't even exist. In this respect, the negative circumstances and events do not really exist on the highest planes. They're just stories we tell ourselves about reality. From this point of view, then, there is nothing to forgive. The only truth is Love. Once we understand this, healing takes place by means of divine grace.

Another way of looking at this is to see that everything in your creation is an opportunity for enlightenment and for your highest good. You've created some of the difficult experiences to pierce you open so that you can emerge fully on the path of light. It is highly likely that the person with whom you believe you had difficulty was a harbinger of good fortune, as the situation brought you to a place of resolution and healing and served as your stroke of awakening.

Whatever may be your way of working with illusion and reality, darkness and light, difficulty and healing—the act of allowing yourself to move on from old unforgiving places in the old cellars and attics of consciousness—there is always the possibility of turning on the light. When this happens, the dark critters that appear to have meandered out from the woodwork all scamper away.

Can I Forgive in This Situation?

A powerful question to ask yourself in any given situation is, "Can I forgive in this situation?" If the answer is no, then continue with whatever phase of the healing process is calling to you. You may need to have some preliminary inner experiences. First you experience; then you release; and next you transform. When and if you're ready, you can move to the next level on your path. Here's how some others have done it.

Carol had the most shocking and intense experience that one can imagine. In her experience, her father had shot and killed her mother and then killed himself. Carol kept this inside herself for a long time. Still, she knew she was holding herself back in life, as she hadn't come to terms with it. In a state of deep relaxation, she heard the voice of her mother telling her that she loved her and that it was okay to release all this now. Carol told her mother that she loved her too. Her Wise Mind told her it was okay to transform her consciousness now, to forgive and be at peace.

Another woman, Julie, also came to a deep level of understanding when she transformed her experience of the sexual abuse by her father when she was very young. After feeling sadness and anger, she released it, and her Wise Mind spoke to her:

> Your mind has been holding onto this and keeping it inside you. Let it dissolve, and see if it's possible for you to release it. You are safe in the highest truth.

She knew then on the deep level of experience that she is safe with the power of the Universe, with the power of God. She was able to experience, release, and transform. She was also able to get to a level of forgiveness through her ability to understand and transform her consciousness. Her Wise Mind told her that she had learned great things from her experience. She'd been deepened, and she knew that her difficulties had been given to her so she could help others to forgive.

Lifting Up a Perception of Reality

It's always possible to turn the light back on and see things from a state of illumination. It's possible to lift up our spirit and our perception with an altered view. The Wise Mind has been given to us for this purpose, as a great guide in the soul that can shift our reality from the illusion of darkness into the reality of light. As the Prayer of St. Francis says, "It is in forgiving that we are forgiven." It is in allowing transformation that we too are transformed.

Chapter Thirty

What Your Wise Mind Might Tell You
#17
You can look at your attachments.

If you desire joy,
Completely forsake all attachment.
By forsaking completely all attachment
A most excellent ecstasy is found.

—The Buddha

The ability to release is a great key in the process of healing. And yet most of us become very attached to things staying the same. Even if we don't experience some things as comfortable, many of us still resist change. Yet change is a constant of human existence. How can we feel more comfortable with change, how can we let go of things and people and ideas, and how can we keep flowing and moving with the great river of life? These are great questions of healing, and the Wise Mind can always assist us with the process.

One of the Buddha's Four Noble Truths is that we become attached to people, fame, money, pleasure, and things of the world, and we cling to these objects, states, and people for dear life. But, the Buddha said, since things are always in flux, we need to allow them to flow. We can understand that such things are transient, and we can learn to go within ourselves where the real treasures lie. It's not that we have to abandon the objects of our desire—relationships, wealth, or fame. We can just let go of our attachment to them.

By contrast, in the realm of the spirit, everything is eternally present.

The Wise Mind and Attachment

The Wise Mind can open us to our innate wisdom by reminding us about our attachments. It might remind us that the human experience is in constant flux and that we'd do well to live in the moment now. We can remember that "all things must pass," and we can allow all things
to flow.

Feeling Totally Loved

Cheryl's husband was twenty-five years older than she was, and he experienced health problems. She looked deeply into this and made contact with her Wise Mind. She felt sadness in her belly and heartache in her soul. She breathed into it and released it. Her Wise Mind said to her,

You're never alone, and you'll never be separated from John. It's just an illusion. You are totally loved. Your connections with John won't end. He'll also communicate with you when he's on the other side. You can now lighten up—lighten up your feelings and your body. No need to worry, to anticipate things about the future. Just be here in lightness and in love.

Her healing words were "I am loved."

The Wise Mind Reminds You

When you go to the essence of yourself and of life, you may understand that there is a natural state of healing that exists within. There is comfort and peace, freedom from grasping and clinging, connection with the Divine. The Wise Mind, as a part of the divine essence, reminds you that all your problems have been answered in this inner place, which is the eternal elixir of the soul.

Chapter Thirty-One

What Your Wise Mind Might Tell You
#18
You are the I AM power.

I AM the Light of the world.

—Jesus, in the Gospel of John

When I say I AM,
I AM setting in motion the limitless power of God.

—Saint Germain, The I AM Discourses

The I AM power is the healing power of the universe. It's the force from which the universe is made, and it is also the basic substance of which you are made. It's the Great Spirit, the God power, the universal substance, the All That Is, the Divine. You came here to lift yourself up toward advanced consciousness. By peeling away layers of illusion that are covering the treasures of love, wisdom, peace, truth, radiance, and light, you can come to know the magnificent consciousness that is your core. This consciousness is the remedy for all the seeming difficulties of ordinary existence. You've come to this earth to dive into this core and to live ultimately in states of enlightenment and wisdom. To unravel the illusion of existence is a journey we are all on.

The I AM power can be experienced as a light or as a profound feeling in the heart or as great wisdom. It is a force field, actually the Force itself, the transcendent power for healing and transformation. When you ask, "What would my Wise Mind tell me about this?" you are activating the I AM power, as wisdom is a part of it. There are other passwords that open this power, such as the words *I AM* themselves. The word *OM* is a form of "I AM" as well. You can use these passwords for life transformation.

You can say, "I AM the power of healing, and I AM healing myself now."

Or, "I AM the Power of Transformation."

Or, "I AM the wisdom, love, and light of the universe."

Or, "I AM the Power and Presence of God."

Using these words is a call to the Universe, to the healing power, to God, asking that the doors be opened to release the awareness of pure and radiant energy into your life.

Transforming Negativities

When you put negativities after *I AM*, as in "I am sick" or "I am a failure," it creates limitation. This is why it is so important to be conscious of the ways you're using language. Through your awareness of when and how you're using negative thoughts and language, you can say, "No, that isn't so. I AM the power of transformation, healing, and love." Whenever you use the words *I AM*, you're opening wide the door of healing, and you're bringing eternal energies into your life. You are the I AM power, and you are filled with enormous capacities for transformation.

I have already mentioned the powerful book called *The I AM Discourses*, channeled materials from the ascended master Saint Germain. The book uses potent and compelling language, and it sounds like this:

The Mighty Energy that surges through your mind into your body is the Pure Electronic Energy of God, the "Mighty I AM presence." If your thought is joyously held upon your God Self as the Source of your Being and Life, that Pure Electronic Energy continues to act unabated, uncontaminated by human discordant qualification.[x]

So you use this power with great intention and love, and you find that it's a manifesting power for healing and light. You can say,

I AM Divine Love.

I AM the Power of Healing.

I AM the Light.

I AM the Wisdom of the Universe.

I AM the Power and Presence of God.

You can call the I AM presence into all of the events of your life, invoking it, thanking it, and loving it. It is the great power of transformation itself.

Transforming the Doldrums into Bliss

Laura had a lot of bills to pay, and her life seemed to be at a standstill. None of her various attempts to push through circumstances in her life or open doors were having any effects at all. She decided to sit down with herself and do the Wise Mind Process. As she paid attention to her inner situation, she felt as if there were a kind of quicksand pulling her down. She breathed into it, and as she exhaled she broke up her experience into tiny molecules and dispersed it. Her Wise Mind began to speak to her:

> You have much to be thankful for. Remember the great abundance you have, and express your appreciation every moment. Give thanks for all you have and all you are. You can handle your situation very well. You are paying all your bills. Take heart, and move into another level of yourself.

Her special healing phrase was "I AM the Life-Transforming Power." This was bubbling with meaning and deep feeling for her. She felt lifted up emotionally and spiritually, and she felt she'd made contact with the Essence. She felt hopeful and positive, and she was able to let go of the heavy burdens that she was carrying as a weight on her shoulders as she continued to repeat, "I AM the Life-Transforming Power." She also became a great power for manifestation, as she had opened up the space for abundance in her life.

The I AM and Self-Esteem

Understanding the great I AM is the answer to self-esteem issues of the personality, as we've already mentioned. When you can reidentify with this great universal power, which is in every fiber of your being, you realize, as Walt Whitman said,

> I . . . am not contain'd between my hat and boots. I am the mate and companion of people, all just as immortal and fathomless as myself. [xi]

When you have this understanding, the old question "Am I good enough?" doesn't have power over you any longer. It becomes "I AM God enough" instead. You always bring your consciousness back to your true Self: "I AM the Life-Transforming Power, the pure light of God."

Linda, an actress in her thirties, always wondered if she were good enough or talented enough. She wondered why people would want to hang out with her. She often got insecure and scared. She paid attention to her experience of not feeling good enough. She breathed into it and exhaled it out, breaking it up into tiny molecules, and it began to abate. Her Wise Mind said to her,

> Focus inward now; slow everything down, and be aware of what's happening. You're okay. The universe is safe. Remember who you truly are. You are a radiant being of the universe.

Linda then had a vision of an angel who told her that she was safe and whole. She felt light in her heart center and the center of her forehead. She knew she was deeply in her power.

Meditating with the I AM

If you'd like, you can sit down in a quiet place and pay attention to your breathing. You can then say to yourself "I" on the in-breath and "AM" on the out-breath. You can keep your focus as long as possible, continuing to bring yourself back to the "I AM" whenever you can. If you like, you can add more to the sentence. You can say, "I AM One with All" or I AM grateful" or "I AM That" or "I AM blessed." You can understand that these are sacred words that are filled with love and affirmation.

All Paths Are Built upon I AM

All mystical revelations, all paths, are based upon the I AM. The Jewish and Christian as well as Eastern paths are all infused with the I AM power. God is often known as the I AM. Rumi, the great Sufi poet, wrote:

> I am neither a Moslem nor a Hindu
>
> I am not Christian, Zoroastrian, nor Jew
>
> My place is the no-place
>
> My image is without face
>
> Neither of body nor the soul
>
> I am of the Divine Whole. [xii]

And Thich Nhat Hanh, the Vietnamese Buddhist monk, asked that he be called by his "true names."[xiii] He was the mayfly and the frog, the child in Uganda, the politician and the oppressed. He knew he was all of these, and in realizing it, he could open to greater awareness of all things.

The Power of the Wise Mind

There is no limit to the power of the I AM and the Wise Mind to heal and transform every aspect of life. "I AM the Life-Transforming Power, and I AM allowing my Wise Mind into every cell of my body, every part of my mind, and every situation in my life." Through your connection with advanced consciousness, you have the ability to live on the highest levels of life.

"As you simply allow

your Wise Mind to speak, you find yourself

moving out of the way so that you can

hear what it has to tell you.

In truth, it's speaking all the time,

and you can become relaxed enough to listen.

Most people can contact the Wise Mind.

It's instinctual."

Part Three

Finding
Your Wise Mind

Chapter Thirty-Two

How Do You Find Your Wise Mind?

Where are you searching for me, friend?
Look! Here am I right within you.
Not in temple, nor in mosque . . .
But here right within you am I.

—*Kabir*

Most people just know it's there. Some know it's there but don't know what to do with it. My eighty-four-year-old Aunt Phyllis was one of the latter. "How can I find my Wise Mind?" she asked me. I told her it was the part of her that knew things, the part of herself that was wise—a simpleminded answer that nonetheless told it like it was.

"Do you mean the wise things that I tell everyone all the time, including myself?" she asked laughingly.

"That's exactly it!" I answered. "You use it all the time—especially when you're telling your grandchildren what you think they need to hear." She knew exactly what I was talking about, and she knew instinctively how to find her Wise Mind.

But What if You Don't Know Where the Wise Mind Is in the First Place?

If it's not second nature or automatic for you to know your Wise Mind, there are some significant things that you can do:

- **You can shift your eyes, soft-focus, and look up while asking your Wise Mind to tell you something.**
  This puts your brain in an alpha state, which is a state of relaxation and which allows new influences to come forth. Have you ever seen one of those books in which you stare at a painting, and as you do, 3-D pictures begin to emerge, and you are invited into a new and magical world? This happens because you go into an altered consciousness via your open-eyed stare, and your perception shifts enough for you to see from another perspective. Truly, it's a form of meditation, and you can invite yourself into these alternate worlds by shifting the position of your eyes: look up, then soft-focus and stare.

- **You can say to yourself, "If I *could* experience my Wise Mind, what might it say?"**
  You will be amazed to see that when you do this, you easily make contact with the Wise Mind. Often we can respond to the hypothetical question more easily than the straightforward one. That's a fascinating phenomenon.

- **You can go into a relaxed state by counting down.** You can count numbers backward very slowly, starting wherever you like—at one hundred or twenty-five or ten. Count very slowly, and close your eyes if you like. Count so slowly that you can fit in words like *I AM* between each number. Then when you get to one, tell yourself that you're completely relaxed, and beckon to your Wise Mind to communicate with you.

- **You can do a special guided relaxation.**
  You can, for example, imagine yourself walking through a wooded area or in a magnificent garden or on a sandy beach. You begin to walk and come upon a cave. Through your curiosity, you peer into the opening of the cave, and you spot a being inside who is friendly and inviting. He or she invites you to come in (or comes to the opening of the cave) and tells you that he or she is a special emissary of the Wise Mind who wishes to give you some wisdom and understanding to bring light to your life. You listen and find out what your Wise Mind would like for you to know about something in your life.

- **You can write it down.**
  You can work with a pen or pencil or with your computer. You can either close your eyes or do an open-eyed stare. At the top of your page, if you like, you can write, "My Dear One," as that's how your Wise Mind may be addressing you, and this can be the trigger for your Wise Mind to appear. You begin to write. At first it may be gibberish or something you already know. As you write, a clarity may come in that surpasses all known understanding. The words may begin to flow as you continue, and when you feel complete, you may emerge from this writing

session with a new perspective on something you've been wanting to understand in your life. You simply ask it to come in and allow it to flow.

- **You can record it.**
  You can use any technology you like to bring forth and record your Wise Mind. You can relax yourself in any of the ways just described, and you can allow the words to flow from you. Again, at first it may sound like nonsense, or it can be something you've already thought about, and as you continue to speak, a fresh understanding comes in. Your heart may open up, as well as your deep understanding of events, and you find yourself in a state of knowing. After you record, you may want to transcribe the words so that you can also get a visual perspective on them.

- **You can allow the voice of the Wise Mind to come from an object.**
  You might want to work with a statue, a doll, a picture, or a memento that is meaningful for you. You can ask a question and listen for an answer, allowing yourself to experience a voice of wisdom speaking to you. Or you can just allow the object to speak forth without asking a specific question. You know, of course, that the "voice" comes from your own consciousness, from the Universe, from the infinite Wise Mind. The external object is simply a tool to assist you in bringing forth this experience.

- **You can invite in a great being to assist you.**
  You can choose a being who is significant to you, such as Christ, Buddha, Moses, Quan Yin, or Saint

Germain. Or you can allow God, Allah, the Beloved, or the Universe to speak wisdom to you. You can open yourself to receive in any of the ways we've talked about above.

- **You can work with another.**
  Sometimes having someone else "hold the space" for you helps to catalyze your own revelations. You can find a professional, or you can work with a friend, and this person can ask your Wise Mind to come forth by saying, "And what would your Wise Mind tell you about that?" If nothing comes, the person can say, "Well, if your Wise Mind *did* speak through you, what might it say?" or "Just imagine that your Wise Mind is speaking through you. What might it be telling you if it were?"

Becoming a Wise Mind Channel

Some people find great revelations and considerable flow as their Wise Mind speaks through them. Some go on and on, often with brilliant truths that gracefully flow from them as they find themselves in a state of trance. Some begin to understand all the perceived difficulties of their lives this way. They look into relationships with their family, friends, business associates. They ask about how to communicate specific issues to these people. They ask about their own business or the state of their finances. They ask about specific health situations and what they need to do to heal themselves. Sometimes they record their answers. Other times they simply go to their computers and write it all down.

When they become proficient, some begin to channel the Wise Mind for others. It's good, of course, to stimulate the abilities of people to communicate with their own Wise Mind, but when there is a truly adept Wise Mind channel, a significant contribution to others can come forth time and time again. Some people are particularly skilled at this channeling, even though they may never have known they had this ability. See what happens to you as you make this transcendent and often sublime connection.

It's Instinctual

As you simply allow your Wise Mind to speak, you find yourself moving out of the way so that you can hear what it has to tell you. In truth, it's speaking all the time, and you can become relaxed enough to listen. Most people can contact the Wise Mind. It's instinctual.

"If you pay attention, breathe,

ask your Wise Mind, and anchor it,

very often you find yourself able to move

from a limited state of consciousness

to a more expanded one."

Part Four

Stories
of the
Wise Mind

Chapter Thirty-Three

Wise Mind Stories

Your original wisdom is as continuous and unstoppable
as the current of a mighty river.
To know whether or not this is true, look inside your own mind.

—Padmasambhava, *The Book of the Great Liberation*

Sometimes the connection with your Wise Mind or the full Wise Mind Process is all you need to transform a situation. Sometimes you need some added ingredients, as we've mentioned in other chapters. Transformation can be clear and simple: If you pay attention, breathe, ask your Wise Mind, and anchor it, very often you find yourself able to move from a limited state of consciousness to a more expanded one.

Let's take a look at how some people (a few stories out of many) have been able to move their awareness from the illusion of darkness into the reality of light.

Becoming Confident in Business

Ellen, a forty-year-old real estate broker, had created some fears in her business, fears that were beginning to paralyze her ability to work. She'd made some investments that didn't work out, and her father had been very critical of her. She was likewise extremely judgmental of herself. She did the Wise Mind Process on one of her main worries—that she wouldn't be able to find commercial real estate space for her clients in the time frame that they needed it. Ellen described the experience: "I have a feeling of anxiety, and my breathing is shallow. I feel it's too big of a challenge; it's insurmountable—especially because I'm not good enough to meet my clients' needs." She breathed into the experience and dispersed it on the exhalation. Her Wise Mind then said to her,

> You're certainly good enough for the clients who come to you. In fact, you're well matched. You're able to help people very well, and it comes to you naturally. You keep your perspective and realize it's a game, and you're very courageous and creative. Stay centered and focused, and remember your greatness.

Her healing word was "perspective." This was refreshing and stimulating for Ellen, and she got back into her work with a more confident and hopeful attitude. Realizing that it was "a game" gave her a new feeling of lightness in her work.

Loving the Family

Michael, a man in his thirties, was estranged from his family for a short while, as he had once erupted in anger at his teenage son. His son had contradicted him one evening, and Michael shoved him, unintentionally scraping his leg on a table. This was the last straw for his wife, who demanded that Michael stay away for a while and put himself in an anger management program because when he got stressed out, he had a hard time controlling himself. He began to do the Wise Mind Process as a part of his healing program. It helped him greatly, but he created in himself a fear of sliding back. He did the Wise Mind Process on this fear.

Michael described the experience: "I have a fear of failure, of becoming an ogre, of causing pain again. My breathing is shallow, and my palms are sweating. I have sinking feelings in my body and mind." He breathed into the experience and dispersed it on the exhalation. His Wise Mind told him:

> It'll be okay. You have enough tools and techniques that'll do the job. In your heart of hearts, you can go back to your family and give them love. You love your kids, and that's the love and respect you'll express to them. A whole new life is happening for you, a better life. Use your new tools, and you'll all be fine.

His healing word was "floating," and it meant being relaxed and lighter than air. He was soon back home, and he had new attitudes and confidence. He wrote and said, "Thank you for the Wise Mind Process. It has helped me relax and take anxiety out of situations. It cleanses my negativities. I breathe out the anxiety three to four times. My Wise Mind then tells me the meaning of my thoughts. Are they unproductive thoughts? Am I being hard on myself? I even do this on an elevator. It's like taking a Valium. It settles me right down."

Creating a Breakthrough in His Mind

Jack, a man of sixty-two, had decided he was a loser. He had gotten off the wheel of his own success fifteen years ago when he lost his position in a company, and he had put his foot on the brake of his life. He now did nothing. He decided that he no longer had any worth, and so his life stagnated. He said he knew he wasn't very good because his parents had told him this over and over. And most important, he had told this story to himself. But Jack knew that the time was up for this pattern, and he was finally ready for a breakthrough. Jack traveled into the terrain of the Wise Mind. As he looked at his situation, he felt weakened and deflated. His Wise Mind spoke to him:

> You don't have to listen to your old thoughts any longer. Begin your life again immediately. Start by cleaning up your home step by step. Pay attention to yourself inside as well, and each day you'll be given the instructions for the daily renewal of your life. If you ever speak negatively to yourself again, say these words: "I don't shop here anymore. I am healing myself now."

Miracles are taking place in Jack's life as he continues to tune in to the frequency of the Wise Mind. He calls this "better than medicine, and healthier too."

Loving Herself

Linda is a nurse in her fifties who was also nursing her own inner growth. Even though she had the demeanor of a peaceful, kind, and loving person, she had created inside a deep sense of herself as unworthy and undesirable. This had been plaguing her in many ways all her life.

She described the experience: "I feel like there's a bug, like a little roach, curled up inside of me. I feel that I'm ugly, and I don't like myself." She breathed into it and dispersed it. Her Wise Mind told her:

> It's the right time now to let go of this discomfort. You are now on the path of healing. This is an old, even ancient, issue inside of you. You are now opening like a bud. All the pain was held in this bud until now. As this bud opens more and more, you release and feel the happiness that's really inside.

Her healing word was "release." She shed many tears, which proved to be the fluids that washed the windows of her soul, and she felt free from this old affliction and was finally able to love herself.

Becoming Happy

Alicia had experienced depression and had been on medication. She perceived many difficulties in her life. She'd been hurt by a breakup of a relationship. Her uncle had also molested her when she was little, and her ex-husband had been abusive. She had a history of misery in relationships. Was there something in her consciousness that might have been manifesting this?

She described the experience: "I feel weak and numb all over, and I can hardly move." She breathed into it and dispersed it. Her Wise Mind told her:

You can heal yourself because you're strong. Remember your grandmother, who always told you that you could be strong. Your grandmother is now giving you courage to move on. You have a whole life to live. Soon you'll be much happier. Give love to the little girl inside yourself, and keep moving on. Come back to your true self, and feel the love that's inside of you.

Her phrase was "I'm strong." She found that she could reduce and then eliminate her medications (with her doctor's assistance), she got a new job, and as she did more and more of this inner work, she felt happier than she had felt in a very long time. After she had done the process a number of times, she was back to work and living productively.

Forgiving and Loving Herself

Sonja thought her friend was doing things that were hurtful, such as coming late to an agreed-upon gathering. She sent her friend an admonishing e-mail about it. Sonja sounded as if she were giving her friend a lecture, and not only that, her friend hadn't been late at all. It was a misunderstanding. Sonja felt like sinking into the floor with guilt, shame, and embarrassment. She apologized profusely, but inside it was difficult for her.

She described the experience: "My heart is sinking down into my stomach. My breathing is shallow. I feel diminished and remorseful, as I had done this once before to the same friend. I feel depressed and sad. How could this have happened? What part of me jumped to conclusions like that and admonished my friend without first finding out the facts?" She breathed into it and dispersed it. Her Wise Mind told her:

> In the same way that you have compassion for your friend, have compassion for yourself. Forgive yourself for your own imperfections. Do something particularly kind for your friend to show her that you care how she feels. Come to the center of yourself. Stay in your center, and come from a place of love. Your own healing power and great intention can turn this into an advantage and opportunity through the power of forgiveness and healing.

Her healing phrase was "I AM the power of healing." Miracles happened with that friend, as Sonja showed her how much she cared. Sonja restored her own sense of balance, and the friendship grew in its strength.

Flying Confidently

Jane had a terrible fear of flying. She and her family planned a trip that would take place very soon, and she wanted the weight of the anxiety to be lifted off her shoulders.

She described the experience: "I feel uncontrollable fear as I think about flying. I feel as if I can hardly catch my breath, and I feel as if my body might fly up in the air at any moment. My feet are tingling." She brought awareness to her breath and began to do the special breathing process. Her Wise Mind told her,

You can control this. You have all the techniques to help you handle it. You've been through fear before, and you're still alive and fine! Going on this trip will give you confidence. You'll survive and be perfectly fine, and you know exactly what to do. You are the great power of the universe, and all is well in your world.

Her phrase was "I am safe and happy." The next week she flew on the plane with ease and grace.

Transforming Emotions

James was separated from his wife. He was also downsized from his corporate job and cared for his two young kids half of the time. Although he was bright, educated, with many skills, he'd been thrown for a loop, and he got anxious throughout his day.

James described the experience: "I feel a general jittery feeling. I notice myself thinking into the future about such things as what I have to do during the rest of the day. My arms and hands are shaking, and there's some fluttering in my stomach. It's a nervous feeling, and I'm taking short quick breaths and breathing shallow breaths." He did the special breathing process. His Wise Mind told him:

You let events throw you off balance—even little things. You dwell on things and let them go over and over in your mind. Despite that, you're stable and grounded. You can break out of your constraints and be free. Take risks, be more daring. You have solid skills and a firm foundation, and you are now finding the right place to put it all into action. Step by step, you're finding your life coming back to you. It's okay to go through this. Your life is transforming now.

His healing phrase was "I let this go, and my life is transformed." He found it easier to handle all that he was going through, and he became more positive and hopeful.

Creating Abundance

Anne, a young artist who makes metal sculptures, struggled with her business. She needed to sell one hundred of her small sculptures each month to make it, and that was not happening. She began to cry in her anguish and frustration; she'd been trying so hard, taking money from her parents, worrying, and feeling powerless.

Anne described the experience: "I feel I'll never make it. I feel defeated, wasted, and tired. I'd like to escape the work, the worry, and the risks." In the same way that her ancestors had wanted to escape the concentration camps of Poland, she wanted to free herself from her own bondage. This was how she told this story to herself, her modern version of the problem. She breathed into the experience and dispersed it on the exhalation. Her Wise Mind told her:

> You've already created a good measure of success. Keep on going. As for what you're feeling now, "This too shall pass. Things worth something are worth risking for." Your friends and family care about you. And within you is strength and healing and love.

Her healing phrase was "I am making it!" From deep within herself, she had renewed her fierce determination and courage, and she kept on going toward her success.

Understanding a Teenage Son

Diane had several children, one of them a nineteen-year-old boy. He got his high school equivalency diploma, and then he stopped everything. He was doing nothing, or so it appeared to his mother, who was extremely aggravated about his inactivity. In her mind he needed to be more productive.

Diane described the experience: "I'm very upset. I feel anxiety throughout my whole body. My mind is 'at the edge.'" She breathed into it and dispersed it. Her Wise Mind spoke to her and said,

> This is his path for now. He may need to stop for a while to figure out where he needs to go. It's for you to release and let go. He'll do just fine.

Her healing phrase was "Let go."

She experienced a remarkable clearing, and her whole being relaxed. This was the beginning of a new relationship with her son.

Releasing a Relationship

Frances had been grieving terribly ever since her fiancé told her that he didn't want to get married. The room had been rented and the cake chosen, the families had met, and one day he told her he "wasn't ready." This came as a cataclysmic shock to Frances, who had no idea that anything like this was going to happen. Her reactions were severe. She described the experience: "I feel like I'm suffocating, out of control. This takes over everything—my body, my mind, and my soul. There's a point in my chest where this won't go away. I feel anxious and powerless." She breathed into it, and it began to melt. Her Wise Mind told her,

> It's time for you to get a life. It's okay to grieve, but if you let go, you can free yourself. Holding on is hard. You are also probably better off. It would have been a difficult life with him anyway, as he has negative qualities. So take yourself back. Take your power back. You are good.

A smile lit up her face, and the relaxation in her body and mind were palpable. She knew that she was on the brink of a new phase of her life in which she was able to leap out of the constraints and illusions of that old relationship and come back to herself.

Compassion toward a Parent

Julie had been quiet about her anger at her father all her life, but one day it was the last straw. She felt her father was cold and unloving toward her, and she wasn't willing to contain it inside any longer. She wrote him a letter telling him that she was angry, but that wasn't enough. She had to take a look inside herself.

Julie described the experience: "I feel a sadness that goes down to the depths of my soul. It's been stuffed down since I was born. I see an image of myself reaching out for some kind of nurturing—love, understanding—but there's nothing there. I need to get my father's presence out of my force field." She breathed deeply into her experience and exhaled. Her Wise Mind said to her:

> Your father is afraid and angry, and you can recreate that picture by now seeing him differently. You can see the love that's at the core of him no matter how it has appeared to you.

Her healing word was "grace." Julie felt great relief and peace. She said she felt like a "happy puppy." Later she looked more deeply into this and found more details about her father's life. She was able to experience a great sense of compassion for him, as well as for herself.

What's Next?

You may remember that there's an optional Bonus Step in the Wise Mind Process. It invites you to ask, "Is there anything else you need to do to heal and transform this?" Many of the people whose stories are told above have combined the Wise Mind Process with deep inner healing. You can read all about deep inner healing, the Transformational Healing Method, in the book *Extraordinary Healing.* [v]

"We've come to this earth to move through

the various challenges that are keeping us from

knowing that we're great, unlimited beings.

Yes, it's possible to remove blinders

from our eyes and move into higher

states of wisdom and love.

If we can fully understand that this

is what we're here to do, we can more fully

accept the challenges in our lives."

Part Five

Wise Mind
Questions and Answers

Chapter Thirty-Four

Wise Mind Questions and Answers

We have to look deeply at things in order to see.

—Thich Nhat Hanh, Peace Is Every Step

In the process of healing and transformation, many nuances and subtleties arise, and some people have questions to ask. It's important to have a good road map as you travel on this vast terrain of human consciousness, so here are some of the questions that arise and well as some answers.

What's the difference between the Wise Mind and the conscious or subconscious mind?

Transformation takes place primarily in the higher mind, the superconscious state. It does involve other levels of consciousness, including the conscious mind and the subconscious. We talked about this in greater detail in chapter 2.

The superconscious is the higher mind, the healing mind—the Wise Mind. It's where the great treasures of our highest potential lie. In it are love, peace, wisdom, light, compassion, and all the greatest healing powers that we've been given as a great gift to transform our lives.

The deep inner mind is the equivalent of the subconscious mind. Here is where the difficulties, the shadows, and the illusions lie. It's actually a vast database that contains everything that you've created in your experience. It also contains the consciousness of all beings, in what Carl Jung called the collective unconscious. We can find out what's inside the deep inner mind by putting it on "search mode," as we would with any database. We can then ask it to show us whatever we may be looking for, be it an antecedent of some circumstance or a particular experience that we'd like to know more about. The deep inner mind is like the "basement" or storage house of our consciousness; it stores the illusions of life.

The conscious mind or everyday mind is the thinking mind. It's the mind that creates grocery lists, changes lightbulbs, and chooses what you'll wear. It has more exalted functions as well, and it's an important component of consciousness, though it too is composed of illusions that we create and call real.

What if I have a hard time describing my situation? What am I supposed to be looking for?

If you're doing the Wise Mind Process and you get stuck on the first step of describing your process, here are a few things you can do:

- If nothing seems to be coming to you, you can say, "If I *did* experience something, what might it be?"

- Or, if you feel you're experiencing nothing, you can say to yourself, "What's that *nothing* like?" You then describe the "nothing" you're experiencing.

- You can ask yourself, "What am I experiencing in my body right now?" You can begin there. You might see if there are particular bodily sensations or experiences in your internal organs. You might look for tightness or discomfort. Then you might take a look at your emotions and see what's taking place. You might pay attention to your breathing and see if it's relaxed or tight. You can even describe thoughts and ideas that come to you. You describe whatever you're experiencing in as much detail as possible.

- Just get into what's going on, and pay attention to whatever is there. Accept what comes, and you will find that the process of looking inside gives you valuable information about what's going on inside yourself.

- You may want to imagine that you can shrink yourself down to a tiny version of yourself, a type of homunculus. Then imagine that in this form you have the capacity to travel inside your own body and experience what's going on inside from the inside out.

- Or you might want to stand back and view your life experience from afar, as if you were the witness. You may see it as a movie, or you might simply be an objective observer. From this vantage point, you can describe your experience in as much detail as possible.

- You can imagine that you're seeing yourself from a skybox, and from this vantage point you have a bird's-eye view of what is taking place in your body and mind.

You can also accept "not knowing," and see where that leads you.

What if I can't see my situation breaking up into tiny molecules?

Many people aren't visual, and it's fine not to be. Being visual is just one of the many modes of experiencing something. If you find that you're not seeing any molecules being dispersed into the universe, you can use another mode of experiencing, one that may be more comfortable for you than visualizing. You may feel it happening, or you might think about it or smell it or just know it's there. You can pretend you see it or just get impressions. No need to actually "see" anything. Just imagine that you do—or just allow yourself to get an impression.

What if emotions come up?

Some people are more comfortable with their emotions than others. Whatever may be your comfort level, feelings such as anger or grief may naturally arise when you're working with the Wise Mind. You can allow this to happen, and instead of pushing your emotions away, you invite them in as you pay attention to them. As you do that, your feelings naturally shift. And as you breathe into them, they shift even more. By the time you ask your Wise Mind about the situation, your feelings have become much easier to handle, and you may find yourself in a state of great relaxation and peace. As you surround yourself with healing and love, whatever comes up in this context is naturally both embraced and dissolved.

There is no need to wallow in your feelings. You can simply allow them to flow, like a mountain stream, until finally there is a point at which there is an opening to great inner understanding. Emotional healing is natural, spontaneous, and deeply healing, though healing can also happen without it. You allow yourself to be present for whatever feelings naturally arise when you do the Wise Mind Process. You're feeling the emotions, and at the same time you're observing them. You're compassionate with your own self, and you ask for the next step of healing to come for you, as you resolve your feelings with wisdom, love, and compassion. If your feelings are intense, you may need to meet with a professional who knows how to allow you to go through your feelings to the other side of them.

It's good to remember that this experience may be what you need for your life learning, and this is what your healing is about for now. The state of witness consciousness is a meditative state that is perfect for doing healing work. To cultivate this, a practice of meditation can be of great value. "Emotions happen," and when they do, it can be a doorway to deep understanding. They are a natural part of human experience, and they can have great value as tools of life education.

How do I know it's really the Wise Mind speaking? How do I know what it's telling me is true?

The Wise Mind is positive and encouraging. If you hear a negative or judgmental voice, it's not the Wise Mind. The Wise Mind is just that—wise. It's a microcosm of the great wisdom of the universe as it's expressed and manifested in you. It's given to us as our birthright as a great "homeopathic remedy of the soul" to heal our negativities, wounds, and difficulties. It's here to lift us up. If you're hearing parental recriminations, words of blame, or judicial pronouncements, it's not the Wise Mind; it's another part of the self.

You know that what your Wise Mind is telling you is true if you sense in your soul that its messages resonate with a very deep place within you. It's not scientifically verifiable. It's something that's felt at the very heart of things. If you hear anything negative when you ask your Wise Mind what it would like to say about your situation, go back and ask again. Listen for encouraging truths that resonate with the highest levels of wisdom. See chapter 4 on the characteristics of the Wise Mind.

When I go deeply inside, I'm afraid I'll find something negative or hard to deal with. What should I do?

We talked about the great poet Rumi, who suggested that we invite in our experiences rather than locking out or rejecting them. It's about seeing our illness and pain as guests. It's about the art of paying attention to the experiences of our life. You pay attention to your wife or husband, your child, your friend, your fear, or your sadness, and they are satisfied. In our culture we like to push things down, get rid of them, banish them, drug them into the oblivion of unconsciousness—but here we're being invited to welcome them all.

Your pain is like a weary traveler on the road. You may feel safe enough to open the door and welcome the traveler in. We talked about this in previous chapters.

Rumi encourages us to welcome and accept what appear to be our difficulties. The moment we do that, the door opens to a deeper life. You can apply this in your own life and in your work, accepting whatever resistance may be present and allowing in the deep feelings that may come through your doors. When you adopt this welcoming and allowing attitude, you can embrace what is here, and it can only serve to expand and enlighten you. Remember that in embracing and loving your experiences, you still don't wallow in them. It's good not to believe that they're your ultimate truth. Some people feel more comfortable looking deeply inside with the assistance or guidance of another, and this can also serve to reassure you.

What if my Wise Mind tells me the wise things to do, but another part of me doesn't want to listen?

My eighty-four-year-old Aunt Phyllis asked me this question: "What if I tell myself wise things from my Wise Brain [that's what she sometimes calls it] but another part of me doesn't want to listen?"

I asked her to give me an example. She said she does it all the time, so it wasn't hard to find an example. "Well, I know this person who is always saying negative things to me about myself, and my Wise Brain tells me to write her off or at least tell her how I feel, but I never do. I just don't listen to the wise things."

I told her that she wasn't the only one who did this. Most of us have created limitations in our minds that have covered over our highest truths. These can be about fear ("What if I do it and they don't like me anymore?") or defeatism ("What's the use?" or a myriad of reasons why it can't or won't work) or force of habit ("Well, I've always done it this way, so it's probably too late to change, and I probably wouldn't know how to change anyway. And change can be scary. I wouldn't know how to be"). We have many illusions that we've created for ourselves that are actually brilliant in the force of their creation but are not really the truth about our lives.

Aunt Phyllis had refrained from listening to her Wise Mind about a lot of things since she was a little girl, and this was in a way a comfort zone for her. She knew that not telling someone how she felt could keep people doing things that weren't for their own or others' highest good and that her reticence to tell them was a way of enabling them. Her not speaking up came out of her own fear. She began to reflect on this and allowed her Wise Mind to speak to her. Her Wise Mind told her that it was time to speak her truth. So she said to the negative person, "You know, this isn't working for me. It's not acceptable anymore." The woman was startled that finally the truth had been spoken. Aunt Phyllis felt empowered, and the woman never spoke negatively to her again.

We look at parts of the self that stand in the way of the truth in greater detail in chapter 20, #7: "Inner resistances can be recognized and transformed."

What if I need to do a lot of deep inner healing?

You may remember that the Wise Mind Process has a possible Bonus Step. This step appears in chapters 5 and 11. If you have a lot to heal, you may want to request the assistance of an inner healer or practitioner. If you choose to do self-healing, you can ask yourself the questions we pose in chapter 2:

Does my inner child need to be attended to?

- Is there some discomfort in my body that I need to address?

- Is there anything that needs to be communicated to anyone?

- Are there some feelings in me that need to be felt and understood?

- Do I need to find out any history or antecedent to my experience?

If you answer yes to any of these questions, you can do the Wise Mind process again as many times as you need to. As you pay attention to anything that is asking for your awareness, you can bring love and wisdom to all parts of yourself. You can, for example, hold your inner child, soothe discomfort in your body, see how you can communicate with wisdom, and make any discoveries you need. Remember that with love and wisdom, you can transform even the most challenging of experiences.

Can this help with physical issues and health situations, like illness, pain, or headaches?

Yes. When you make contact with the Wise Mind, there is always the potential of shifting matter and transforming what appears as illness. The mind, together with the powers of higher consciousness, can create great physical shifts. Of course, you make certain that you're in touch with a doctor or healing practitioner if you do have physical issues that need attention.

The mind is electromagnetic. It has magnetism and vibration, and it can magnetize or draw in healing events via healing thoughts. This is how it can shift matter. You make contact with your own intrinsic healing, and you generate great healing power. A man named Bob was diagnosed with cancer. He realized he was living with great stress and everyday anger, and his Wise Mind told him that in shifting his attitude, he could make great changes in his body. His Wise Mind told him to go more deeply into meditation, to understand the mental healing process more fully, and to be in touch with his spirit. He needed to strengthen his natural spiritual connection. This, in addition to visualizing the cancer cells shrinking and visualizing his radiation as healing beams of light, helped him to live many more years past his allotted time. He also began to understand the ultimate reality of his inherent wholeness. As his Wise Mind had prompted, he changed his lifestyle. He also found his inner guide, and he knew he was on the road to healing.

If you have a headache or another physical issue, see how the Wise Mind Process can help you. By focusing awareness on these experiences, you can move and shift them.

Look also at the understanding of illness as a creation of consciousness. Can we recreate circumstances with our minds? This may or may not be easy for us to do, as the solidity of matter is very compelling; yet it is always an approach that we may want to consider.

Can I do this work with someone else— with a family member or mate? What if he or she won't do it?

Some friends and mates would love to work with you. They'll jump at the opportunity. Others are very reluctant. For some, it upsets the roles they've set up in their relationship with you. Some seem to think that it puts you above them if you take the role of the healer. They're not comfortable with this setup. Others don't want you to seem to control them, and even though you're not doing that, they may interpret it that way. Another issue for some is that you have close relationships with certain people—your children, mates, and others—and your own issues may cloud the clarity of the experience.

Nevertheless, there may be absolutely no problems working with others you know. It may be a smooth and natural process, and nothing will get in the way of what you can do together. You may want to work with one another, if you like. You'll know who is open and who is resistant. It's wise not to push the river, not to attempt to push anyone into a healing situation if that doesn't flow naturally. If you know that the person absolutely doesn't want to do this with you, you may want to stand back gracefully and allow this to be okay.

How can I do this work with a group?

One idea in working with groups is to use the Wise Mind Truths ("What Your Wise Mind Might Tell You") as the basis of the work you do together. You can choose to do one Wise Mind Truth each week, if you like. You can read each one aloud and allow others to see what arises in them from their own deep experiences. They can share what they're experiencing, and then you can do the Wise

Mind Process with them to release and transform their experiences. You can do the meditations with the group, allowing them to share what is going on within them.

How can I do this work as a healing practitioner?

If you're a professional, you can use the Wise Mind Process with the issues of any client. If you're a hypnotherapist, you can use the process both before you go into hypnosis and during the hypnosis itself. If you're a psychologist or psychotherapist, you can use the Wise Mind Process with or without inducing a state of relaxation. It can flow with any work you do together. It can assist you in creating results with most clients.

What if I need to tell someone how I feel, to communicate my grievances? What if I need to work out an issue with someone and not just myself?

If you and the other person would like, you can do the Wise Mind Process together. Or you can ask your Wise Mind to tell you an effective way of communicating with the other person. You can also find out through the Wise

Mind what the truth of the situation might be. This would assist you in coming to the situation with greater understanding and compassion, and it would help you to get an overview of what's taking place between you. It would keep you in a greater state of wisdom and objectivity. Then you can communicate what you've learned from your own Wise Mind, and you can then together make the necessary shifts in your lives.

What if it doesn't work for me?

You can do the Wise Mind Process several times and see if the repetition helps. You can also see if you need to shift the issue that you work on. Perhaps it needs to be more specific. See if you can redefine the issue from different angles. For example, if you're working on anxiety, see if you can make it more specific by working on the feeling in the pit of your stomach instead. Perhaps you need to spend more time on any of the four steps, for example, taking more time to do the breathing.

Another way that you can approach this is to do the Bonus Step, which you'll find in chapters 5 and 11. The material here will guide you to some other aspects of deep inner healing, such as loving the child (or any other part of the self) within you.

If you're having difficulty experiencing your Wise

Mind, see above tips for finding it more easily. If you're having difficulty doing this on your own, find a practitioner who can assist you.

I want to heal and transform, but I have so many obstacles. I feel that something is in my way. What can I do?

If you feel that obstacles are blocking your path, you can first see and experience the limitation in your life. You can appreciate it as a brilliant creation of your consciousness, in the same way that a movie director might stand back and view his or her story saying, "How amazing that I could have created this!" Then you can move into greater expansion and freedom. We keep limitations often because of perceived secondary gains ("If I keep this weight, no men will bother me") or fears ("If I get a new job, I might fail to do well") or conditioned considerations ("If I do that, I'll be better than my mother or father or brother"). You have to want to go beyond these considerations more than you want to hold onto them.

Inside many people create limiting thoughts, like, "I'll never make it. It's too uncomfortable out there. If I succeed, I'll be scared. If I fail, I'll know for certain that I'm the failure I always thought I might be." We have made up these messages, and they serve as limitations. Many of us allow these voices to dominate our existence.

Some of us, however, look for ways to break free. You may ask, "What would my Wise Mind tell me about this?" Your Wise Mind might tell you something like this:

> First love the limiting force, and then you can create a breakthrough. You're ready to expand your level of living. Appreciate all that the limiting force has done for you, and appreciate your power in creating such a strong experience inside, and now reaffirm that you are the power and presence in your own life. Now you can find freedom.

Obstacles are not, in and of themselves, bad. They are mechanisms that you've created inside yourself, that you have thought would take care of you. Everything in life is an opportunity for awakening to your greatness and your strength as well as to the underlying energy of love and healing in the universe. Here is a technique you can use to find the obstacle:

Ask yourself to finish this sentence: "I don't want to ____(here you name the positive experience that you say you want to do or feel) because . . . " Then you fill in the reason. You keep asking yourself questions until you reach the root of what's bothering you. Here is an example:

> I don't want to let go of my fear because . . .
> I feel it's protecting me.
> And I need that protection because . . .
> Because I don't feel safe.
> And I don't feel safe because . . .
> Because I was hurt before, and I think I'll be hurt again.

So here you have your issue: You believe that you're protecting yourself. Here's an opportunity to do some great transformation, using the Wise Mind Process and bringing love to all aspects of your self and your experience.

You can read about this in greater detail in chapter 20: "What Your Wise Mind Might Tell You #6: Inner Resistances Can Be Recognized and Transformed."

What if similar situations keep coming up in my life?

The "frozen pictures in the soul" that we talked about in chapter 18 may be asking to be healed and transformed.

If you find that patterns continue to arise within you, you may want to look deeply within and ask your Wise Mind if there is a particular part of you that needs to be paid attention to. If you find this to be the case, reread chapter 18, "What Your Wise Mind Might Tell You #5: You're the Way You Are, Not the Way You Were," and do the Wise Mind Process, looking at how you might give this part of yourself the gift of healing and transformation. Look at how you might speak the truth to the illusions of your mind.

I know I'm a healer, but I've had such a difficult life, and I'm not perfect. Can I still help others?

In chapter 19 we talked about the archetype of the wounded healer, and we looked at how you've created your difficulties to mold you into a healer through the process of great inner growth. If you've had a challenging life, reread chapter 19, "What Your Wise Mind Might Tell You #6: Perceived Wounds Can Pierce You Open," and look at the deepening process that comes through challenges and how it has contributed to the work you've come to do in this world. Your Wise Mind can assist you in finding ways to awaken. What you eventually come to understand is that now you have the opportunity to dissolve an old part of your personality, an old way of being, and through your connection with higher consciousness, you emerge as someone new. You follow the process of transformation and allow it to work for you in your life. You gain empathy for others who are ill. And you also gain a special inner quality that is the mark of a transformed life. The fact that you've had challenges in your life can make you a compassionate and wise healer.

What if I do the Wise Mind Process and more and more issues come up?

It's normal for more issues to be uncovered as you work them through. It's like digging in the sand on the beach when you were a child, finding shells or glass as you dig, and knowing that you are finding treasures on the way to reaching the "other side of the earth." It's also like the small toys we used to have in which a doll or an egg rested inside another doll or egg, and we could keep on opening them to find more and more. We often resolve an issue, and then it opens the door to something on an even deeper level. We can consider our healing work successful when this happens, as we're diving even deeper into the essence of things, and we're getting closer and closer to the ultimate truth—that we are made of the substance of the universe and that we are the eternal Self in our highest essence. The more layers you peel off, the deeper you go to finding out the core of all that is. Keep on doing the Wise Mind Process with each issue, and consider doing some of the extra steps also that we mentioned above.

Do I need to find the root cause of my issue in order to heal and transform it?

No, you can heal and transform your issue on any level that's right for you. When you involve the healing wisdom of the higher self, you can see things so differently that you may be able to transform your issue in the twinkling of an eye. It's often interesting to find out what might be the seeming cause of a particular challenge in your life. But it might just "seem" to be the cause, as the true cause of all issues is separation from the love and wisdom of the universe. We already looked at this in chapter 22, "What Your Wise Mind Might Tell You #9: The True Root Cause of All Your Issues Is Separation from the Infinite Source."

Is it really possible to heal?

Becoming healed and whole is what we're doing here on earth, transforming the illusion of darkness so that we can ultimately become enlightened beings. This means that we've come to this earth to move through the various challenges that are keeping us from knowing that we're great, unlimited beings. Yes, it's possible to remove blinders from our eyes and move into higher states of wisdom and love. If we can fully understand that this is what we're here to do, we can more fully accept the challenges in our lives. They are obstacles to transform rather than albatrosses around our necks. They are the gifts that have been given to us so that we can move to higher and higher states of awareness and understanding.

"Your Wise Mind

may assist you in making a decision,

or it may soothe or even remove a

difficulty and help you to

understand it more fully."

Part Six

Create
Your Own
Inner Wise Mind
Workshop

Chapter Thirty-Five

Create Your Own Inner Wise Mind Workshop

Take stock of yourself and your habits,
And find out what is standing in your way. . . .
You must know yourself as you are.

—Paramahansa Yogananda, *Where There Is Light*

You may want to take some time out from the busyness of your life to transform, heal, and get in touch with the radiance of your being. Find a good place for this, where you're not likely to be interrupted (though if you are, it's all right too). Find a place that makes you feel relaxed, and consider it, if you like, to be a sacred space. It may be a corner of a room or at a table or desk or outside in a natural setting. Any place that you designate as a sacred space will do.

Bring with you a special notebook, which could be a Wise Mind notebook, and a pen or pencil. Or you can use a computer. Close your eyes for a moment, and just get present. To do this, you may want to concentrate on your breathing and stay with it as consistently as you can. If your breathing is rapid, your awareness of it will help it to become more peaceful and natural.

In this transformational space, you can do any of the meditations in chapter 36 first, if you like.

Then you can do any of the following:

Tell a Story of Something in Your Life from a Transformed Perspective

In your notebook or in your mind, take a different point of view toward something that has taken place in your life, and tell a story about it. Take a transformational point of view in which you see the great overview from the vantage point of the Wise Mind. Here are some examples:

The old way would be: "My wife left me, and I was filled with grief, and it ruined my life and took everything I had." The Wise Mind way would sound like this: "I had a great fierce teacher who came into my life and opened the possibilities by freeing me to be able to go on my path of healing. And though it seemed to be very painful at the time, I know as I look at it now that it was a great transformational experience. It gave me a sense of my own power. I realized that the true reality is love, and I opened myself to see the love in everything."

We think the first way is the reality because it's so deeply ingrained in us. But when we look more deeply, there is a more profound truth. An even more profound truth in this situation is that it may have happened only in the province of the mind, and it may not be the true reality. That's the "skybox" perspective.

Another example: "When I was pregnant, I was engaged to a man who didn't want me to have my daughter, and he left me when I was pregnant because he didn't want to have a baby. He wanted me to choose between him and her. So for a long time, I was very angry and very hurt."

The Wise Mind way: "Even though it didn't work out between us, he gave me the gift of my daughter. Because he left me, I was able to meet my husband when my baby was about ten months old. I'm thankful that this brought me to a place where my husband and I are so much more compatible, really soul mates, and the gift is my daughter. I no longer feel angry or hurt about the other man. I forgive and let it go." Another point of view: "This is something that is not real. The reality is that I was and am the power and presence of God."

One more example: "When I was seventeen years old, I was raped in the streets. This was the most shocking, hurtful experience of my life, and it just about ruined things for me in every way. I felt so much fear and lack of freedom, and I blamed myself."

The Wise Mind way: "At seventeen when I was raped, I was given a very fierce lesson. I was able to work through it, and knowing how difficult it is to do that, I found out it was possible, and with that knowledge, I'm able to help other people. This has given me a gift of a greater depth than I would have had otherwise, and it has filled me with compassion and understanding." Or from the High View, "This is a story I've been telling myself for a long time. If I go to the highest vantage point, everything is filled with love."

Take a moment, if you would, and tell a story from your own life that comes from the wisdom and truth of your Wise Mind. You'll be able to see old experiences of your life in a new and transformational way.

Channel Your Wise Mind

Sit down with a pen and paper or keyboard, or even a microphone, and allow yourself to become relaxed. You can pay attention to your breathing or count down from ten to one slowly. As you're relaxing, you may want to tell yourself, "I'm now becoming a vehicle for my Wise Mind to come through me. I open to receive information and wisdom from my Wise Mind. I am a channel for the great Wise Mind."

You may have a question you want to ask, or you may just want to listen and experience the guidance and wisdom that come forth. You may ask for wisdom about a current relationship, a career decision, a financial issue, a challenge in the life of someone else, or a difficulty in the world. Your Wise Mind may assist you in making a decision, or it may soothe or even remove a difficulty and help you to understand it more fully.

As you relax, you may be able to experience a type of open-eyed trance and write some wisdom and guidance onto a piece of paper or into a computer. Let it just come through your arms, into your hands, out your pen or keyboard, and onto the page or screen. Become a vehicle for this writing. Just as a dancer can dance without thought, a musician can play without thought, you can write without thought. Just let it come through. Again, you may want to pose a question, or you may just wish to listen to wisdom. If you receive nothing but relaxation, consider that a very peaceful state to receive. Feel free to invent your experience or even to make up the wisdom more actively, as this too comes from the divine imaginal realm.

Sometimes your messages will be short and general, such as, "You're going in the right direction. You're finding what you're looking for. Be strong, have patience and fortitude, and the seeds you have planted will flower." Some messages will be more detailed, telling you specifically what's happening in your relationships, your finances, or your work life, and then you may receive messages about how to improve and transform your situation. You may also be reminded that what you've perceived as true for so long is not the ultimate truth, and you can then feel free to expand into your true self.

See if there is a trigger word for stimulating the flow that you can use in future trance writing. It may be that you write "My Dear One" at the top of the page. Or you can write a greeting, like, "Hello." Trust that your guidance, whether visual or aural or written—or in any other form—is the voice of your Wise Mind. The voice of the Wise Mind will always be uplifting and from the realms of light. Your Wise Mind might become a guide or an angel, or it might just remain the clear voice of wisdom. You may want to write a question or an issue at the top of your message, or you may simply begin writing and let your Wise Mind speak to you.

If nothing comes forth from your Wise Mind, open up the flow of words by writing anything, even if at first it seems like nonsense or gibberish. Reaffirm that you're bringing forth a message from your Wise Mind, and you may find that before long something of value ultimately comes through you.

As you write or speak into a microphone, stay as relaxed as possible, and let the words flow as easily as possible. You may be amazed at the quality of the wisdom and information that comes from your Wise Mind. It may tell you something very specific, such as, "You're going to leave your job next month and move to Nevada." Or it may be very general, like, "You're on the right path. Keep up the good work." Or you may hear words of truth: "You are the love of the universe." You might get an image instead of words. Trust that you have access to the great Wise Mind, and allow its message to come through you at any opportunity.

When you've finished bringing forth the message, see if there is anything else that your Wise Mind wishes to channel through you, and if not, bring yourself back by counting up from one to five, making your inner voice louder as you reach five. Suggest to yourself that you will emerge from relaxation feeling energized and inspired.

Do the Wise Mind Process

The Wise Mind Process is a four-step transformational process for turning your life around. It's based on the principles of Experience–Release–Transform. First *experience* what's going on with you; then *release* it; next *transform* it through the power of the Wise Mind. Reread chapters 4 through 11 to find out how to do it. If you use the Wise Mind Process to transform your issues as they come up in your life, you will truly make significant shifts. You can use it to overcome stage fright, writer's block, fear of flying, problems in relationships, pain, stress, grief, anger, and any of the myriad of issues and illusions that are a part of the human condition.

You can begin a journal of your work with the Wise Mind process, chronicling your inner transformations step by step.

Reread Each Wise Mind Truth, and See What It Has to Say for Your Own Life

Write or type your own responses to each of the Wise Mind Truths, and see what each one is saying specifically to you. Look deeply at how each one can be applied to the details of your own path. Then see how you can transform your previous experiences so that you can move to the next level of your consciousness. You may want to again use the Wise Mind Process. You can use parts of it, or you can do the entire process.

"You are transformed by the power of transformation itself, the Great Spirit within you. You are whole, complete, powerful, perfect at the very essence of your being, and you can go deeply within on a regular basis to touch in to this great power, which can help you to overcome all of the challenges of life.
You are, in fact, the power of transformation itself. You are that power."

Part Seven

Meditations
and Scripts

Chapter Thirty-Six

Meditations and Scripts

You can read the following meditations to relax and remind yourself of the messages inside, and you can also record them for yourself. If you're a practitioner, you can use them for classes and with clients; see instructions for this on the next page.*

Whenever you work with meditations and scripts, it's important to be in a relaxed state when you deliver them, whether it's to yourself or anyone else. You read them very slowly in as relaxed a voice as possible. Make sure you pause long enough to give your listener (or yourself) time to experience whatever is suggested. When there is counting involved, as in relaxing by counting backward, count very, very slowly. The more relaxed your voice is, the more relaxed your listener will be. Whether this listener is yourself or someone else, it's important to maintain a steady, slow pace. This will slow your breathing and calm your nervous system, and it will help you to reach deeper states of relaxation so that you or another can get into the process and hear what you're saying.

As you read the meditations, see how deeply you can get into the content. This will give you a deep and transformational experience. Notice that when you relax, you count numbers backward. When you come back, you count forward, and your voice also becomes louder. The more you get into the experience, the more you get out of it.

Let yourself go on a beautiful journey into higher consciousness.

* These scripts are copyrighted. You can read them to classes or clients, but you cannot sell them. Whenever you do use them, please give credit to Marilyn Gordon. Thank you.

MEDITATION ON
The Essence of Your Being

Just get nice and comfortable now, and let yourself relax completely. Take a deep breath in and exhale, and as you do, just let go and relax. Let your mind relax and all your thoughts, and let your body relax and all your muscles, nerves, and bones. Take another deep breath in, and exhale once again, and let a peaceful wave of relaxing energy wash over your body and mind, relaxing you completely. Pay attention to your breathing, and as you do, just allow yourself to relax even more deeply. And as you pay attention to your breathing, I'm going to count from 10 to 1, and you can just allow yourself to relax even more. And as I count, if thoughts come, just let them come and then let them go—as if they're birds or clouds just floating across the sky. . . . 10 . . . 9 . . . 8 . . . 7 . . . 6 . . . 5 . . . 4 . . . 3 . . . 2 . . . 1 . .

And now, just pull your awareness deep inside, way beyond all the layers of your outward personality. Just bring yourself deeply inside to the essence of yourself. In this essence, there's wisdom, peace, love, light, compassion, forgiveness, and the ability to stand back to be the witness of all things. In this essence, you know that everything is connected, because everything has a spark of life within it. Everything is composed of dancing molecules of life itself. And because everything has that same life in it, everything is related to everything else. And this great power within is also the power of transformation, and you can make contact with it. You may want to see if there's a word, an image, or a phrase that helps you to connect with this great transformational life force power. You might see an image or feel a feeling or hear some words—something that can connect you with the supreme life force. (pause.) And you can imagine yourself imbued with that force, whole and complete, having transformed your life. It might come as a picture, a feeling, words, or as an impression. (pause.) You are transformed by the power of transformation itself, the Great Spirit within you. You are whole, complete, powerful, perfect at the very essence of your being, and you can go deeply within on a regular basis to touch in to this great power, which can help you to overcome all of the challenges of life. You are, in fact, the power of transformation itself. You are that power. That power is you. So let yourself once again bring back that representation for your essence that came to you a few moments ago—see it or feel it, hear it, or just know it's there. And once again, know that you are whole, powerful, perfect, at your very core—and that's the essence of you as a being. That is the basis for your own self-esteem—to know who you are in the very deepest highest sense. "I AM whole, powerful, perfect, abundant, alive, and filled with awareness, consciousness, and bliss. I AM the life force itself." And so you can now just be with this; allow it to center and ground you, allow yourself to incorporate this into your idea of who you are. . . .

Coming back with a sense of high self-esteem, profound connection with the essence of life itself—with strength and love and all good things. Coming on back now. . . . 1 . . . 2 . . . 3 . . . 4 . . . and 5.

© Marilyn Gordon, 2007

MEDITATION ON
Your Transformational I AM Power

Just get nice and comfortable now, and let yourself
relax completely. Take a deep breath in, and exhale, and as
you do, just let go and relax. Let your mind relax and all
your thoughts, and let your body relax and all your
muscles, nerves, and bones. Take another deep breath in,
and exhale once again, and let a peaceful wave of relaxing
energy wash over your body and mind, relaxing you
completely. Pay attention to your breathing, and as you
do, just allow yourself to relax even more deeply. And as
you pay attention to your breathing, I'm going to count
from 10 to 1, and you can just allow yourself to relax
even more. And as I count, if thoughts come, just let them
come and then let them go—as if they're birds or clouds
just floating across the sky. . . . 10 . . . 9 . . . 8 . . . 7 . . . 6 . .
. 5 . . . 4 . . . 3 . . . 2 . . . 1 . .

Know that as you relax, you're able get in touch with
the transformational power at the core of your being. And
know that every moment of your life is an opportunity to
transform your consciousness, to drop all you thought you
were and jump into a new level of understanding. And so,
if you would, just allow yourself to get in touch with the
radiant power of the universe in any way that you're able.
It may be that you experience yourself as a source of light
with beams coming forth from you—or you may want to
imagine the beams of the universe beaming upon you.
(pause.) Within you are wisdom, light, love, peace, truth,

awareness, understanding, and healing power. You are whole, powerful, perfect, radiant, illumined, great, and free.

You affirm to yourself: "I AM the healing power of the universe, and I AM transforming my life with my consciousness now. I release obstacles to my greatness. I release my limitations. I'm not who I was. I AM who I AM. I can watch my life and thoughts from the state of the witness. I have the ability to shift my consciousness at any moment. I dissolve old obstacles. I remove the blinders from my consciousness. I remind myself of my oneness with the One. I have compassion for all people, all beings, and at any moment, I have the ability to move my consciousness into states of empowerment, radiance, peace, and truth."

You allow yourself to relax even more deeply now. And if there's anyone or anything in your life that has seemed challenging to you, just tell yourself that you can move beyond this now. You can move to a state of radiance and illuminating power. You're in a state of transformation. You can move on to be fully your own being, your own self. You are the great healing power. You are the great transformational power, and your mind is creative and brilliant. So just take a moment now to listen to whatever your own Wise Mind would like to tell you about this. (pause.)

And now you can say: "With the wisdom of my higher self, and the power of my healing mind, I AM transforming my life now. All the cells of my body, all the powers of my mind, are transforming me now." And now you may want to imagine yourself as healed and whole, powerful and perfect, strong, prosperous, coming from the center of yourself. See it or feel it or hear it—or just know that it's there. "I AM the power of transformation. I AM the power of healing, and I AM transforming my life now. I have the ability to shift my awareness at any time. I AM love, I have love, and I AM loved. I AM the power of love itself. I shine like a million suns. I AM the power of light itself. Within me is luminous radiance. I illumine this world as I walk through it. Within me is wisdom and knowledge. I come to this world with understanding, and I walk the path of enlightenment and self-realization, becoming stronger and stronger, more and more powerful. With the wisdom of my higher self and the power of my healing mind, I am healing and transforming my life right now. I AM whole, powerful, perfect, abundant, loving, and I AM the transformational power itself."

So in your mind's eye, in any way that you can—it may come visually, or through your hearing or thinking—just imagine yourself in your highest and greatest state, doing what you enjoy doing, something that you came here to do. Imagine yourself doing, being, having whatever you'd like. Go ahead and let it shine. You are the power of transformation, and your life is growing and expanding. Your life is a radiant life, and you live it with wisdom, knowledge and understanding and love, and all good things.

And if you like, you can see another detail of your life in its fullest, in its highest. See it, feel it, know it, experience it as fully and deeply as you can, for that is you, your radiant self. And if there's something you wish for a loved one, just send a thought form in the direction of a loved one. Perhaps it is healing, perhaps it is abundance, perhaps it is forgiveness—whatever you'd like it to be. Send it in the direction of a loved one—or two or three—and know that through the love you have in your heart and the brilliance you have in your intention, your loved one receives your good wishes. As you become stronger and stronger, power comes to you, not power over, but inner power and strength, the ability to do things skillfully, the ability to be your very greatest self. And you have the ability to create transformation. All is well in your world. You are the power of transformation, and you are healing and transforming your life right here and right now.

And so, you can come back now, and you can bring with you the peacefulness and the power and the love that you have from inside. You can bring these qualities back to the outer. Coming back—feeling very strong, alert, peaceful, and free. Feeling rested and energized, with a sense of well-being, joy, aliveness, and peace. Coming on back now . . . 1 . . . 2 . . . 3 . . . 4 . . . and 5.

© *Marilyn Gordon, 2007*

MEDITATION ON
Knowing True Self-Worth:
Experiencing Your Radiant Self

Just get nice and comfortable now, and let yourself relax completely. Take a deep breath in, and exhale, and as you do, just let go and relax. Let your mind relax and all your thoughts, and let your body relax and all your muscles, nerves, and bones. Take another deep breath in, and exhale once again, and let a peaceful wave of relaxing energy wash over your body and mind, relaxing you completely. Pay attention to your breathing, and as you do, just allow yourself to relax even more deeply. And as you pay attention to your breathing, I'm going to count from 10 to 1, and you can just allow yourself to relax even more. And as I count, if thoughts come, just let them come and then let them go—as if they're birds or clouds just floating across the sky. . . . 10 . . . 9 . . . 8 . . . 7 . . . 6 . . . 5 . . . 4 . . . 3 . . . 2 . . . 1 . .

And as you relax this deeply, you look inside yourself, and you find your true worth and magnificence. You're an extraordinary being, filled with radiance and the good of the entire universe. Inside you is an infinite flower, which never stops being beautiful. You can go more deeply into your truth, and you can identify yourself with something great, something eternal that makes you realize the true beauty that flows from inside you.

Love and appreciate yourself for all the creative power that you demonstrate in your life. Love and honor yourself for all that you've been able to do and be and have. Love yourself because you exist as the power and presence of the Universe. Love your true nature, your radiant Self. Let yourself experience that love in your heart.

Now, imagine the lines of your limited physical self blurring as you merge with all existence. The molecules that comprise your body are the same molecules that manifest the entire universe. That is the truth of "I AM One with All That Is." The lines of old limits are released, and you become at One. Know deep inside yourself that this understanding can transform your daily issues. Your Wise Mind can guide you to a transformed existence. Imagine identifying with this expanded state of being, your true Self.

You identify yourself with something greater, something eternal, something that expands your entire ground of being. You are beyond limitation. The world of the light is infinite. You are free to be your greatest Self.

Just imagine yourself with light all around you. You are radiant and alive. Your Wise Mind guides you to the path of healing and ultimate enlightenment. You are opening your consciousness and heart. Let yourself expand even more now. You may experience yourself as a part of the universe, the planetary system. You are illuminated by light and centered in peace. Whatever you experience, it is good. You know your true self, and your true self is always magnificent, radiant, great, and wise. You are now expanding and merging with the universe, releasing your limits and allowing your magnificence to shine. You are great power and love.

And so, you can get ready to come back to the ordinary world now. You can get ready to bring your expanded self into the world, and you can bring with you the light and the power and the love that you have from inside. You can bring these qualities back to the outer experience. If you're ready to come back now, you can allow yourself to feel very strong, alert, peaceful, and free. Feeling rested and energized, with a sense of well-being, joy, aliveness, and peace. Coming on back now . . . 1 . . . 2 . . . 3 . . . 4 . . . and 5.

© *Marilyn Gordon, 2007*

MEDITATION ON
Your Transformational Power of Love

Just get nice and comfortable now, and let yourself
relax completely. Take a deep breath in, and exhale, and as
you do, just let go and relax. Let your mind relax and all
your thoughts, and let your body relax and all your
muscles, nerves, and bones. Take another deep breath in,
and exhale once again, and let a peaceful wave of relaxing
energy wash over your body and mind, relaxing you
completely. Pay attention to your breathing, and as you
do, just allow yourself to relax even more deeply. And as
you pay attention to your breathing, I'm going to count
from 10 to 1, and you can just allow yourself to relax
even more. And as I count, if thoughts come, just let them
come and then let them go—as if they're birds or clouds
just floating across the sky. . . . 10 . . . 9 . . . 8 . . . 7 . . . 6 . .
. 5 . . . 4 . . . 3 . . . 2 . . . 1 . .

And as you relax this deeply, you come to know that
inside of you is the very source of love, and it is a gift
within you to nourish, heal, and transform your entire life.
Now you can open up the doors and windows in your
soul so that you can feel the great qualities of the power
of love. Love exists in you independent of any external
source. It's the essential substance of the universe. You
might experience it as feelings of deep caring, as ecstasy,
as a divine force field, or as a transcendent healing power.
Molecules of love are moving in every cell of your being.
So let yourself experience those dancing molecules of
love. You may feel them, see them, or just invent them
with your mind. Any way that you're able to give them

life is fine. And just know that it's okay not to feel them at all, but to just think about the possibility that you are permeated with the spirit of love, whether it is apparent or not. Love is still always present. Today is your chance to experience its presence. Today is your day to experience more love.

Just imagine that there is an ocean of love both inside you and surrounding you, as well as everything else in the universe. It's vibrating with a beautiful flowing energy that has the ability to heal and uplift everything it touches. It moves into and through you, especially through your heart, and it has the ability to move away anything that's unlike itself. You are healing any old difficulties of life and thoughts with this flowing energy of love.

You can allow the love to move through and from you as a great universal flow, knowing that your essence is made of love. (pause.)

If you like, you can imagine someone or something who has great love and carries the love vibration. This can assist you in opening your own. It might be a great radiant being who can open you to the experience of love. It might be a friend or relative, past or present, alive or passed on, who has an open heart and can open you up to knowing the expanded power of love. It might be a beloved animal. Just allow yourself now to experience this catalyst, and see how it can expand and deepen your own flow of the energy of love. You may feel uplifted or transported, or you many feel nurtured and comforted, or you may feel totally transformed. You may experience all of these. (pause.)

You may now want to give love to your own self. Just go ahead and bring love to yourself now or at any age. Experience the loving energy. Experience your own expansion as you are infused with this great inner power. The love can emanate from another person or a great being, or it can be from the universe, from God, from the power of love itself. Let the love open and expand you. You might experience it as human love, or it may be a great radiant, dynamic, blissful universal force. Experience this love as a great gift to you from the universe. You can hold your life in the high-frequency vibration of love, and you can actually shift your entire experience here.

You can allow your Wise Mind to speak to you of love, to tell you anything it would like to tell you about love. Just take a moment, and allow yourself to get in touch with the loving voice of your Wise Mind. You might hear it or feel it or see it or just know it's there. (pause.)

With an opening heart, you can see that there is a loving force that is propelling this world. You can see that you're empowered and that the love is there always—even if you're not aware of it at any given moment, even if there's no one else there to give or receive love. As you listen to these words, let your heart remain open:

> It's in every one of us to be wise.
> Find your heart; open up both your eyes.
> We could all know everything without ever knowing why.
> It's in every one of us, by and by.

Love is the basic energy of the universe, the core of energy in every molecule and cell. This energy permeates every part of you. Love is what you came here on earth to know.

And so, you can get ready to come back to the ordinary world now. You can get ready to bring your loving and loved self into the world, and you can bring with you all the energy that you have within. You can bring your expanded qualities back to the outer experience. If you're ready to come back now, you can allow yourself to feel loved, loving, strong, alert, peaceful, and free. Feeling rested and energized, with a sense of well-being, joy, aliveness, and peace. Coming on back now . . . 1 . . . 2 . . . 3 . . . 4 . . . and 5.

© *Marilyn Gordon, 2007*

MEDITATION ON
the Power of Light to Illuminate and Heal

Just get nice and comfortable now, and let yourself relax completely. Take a deep breath in, and exhale, and as you do, just let go and relax. Let your mind relax and all your thoughts, and let your body relax and all your muscles, nerves, and bones. Take another deep breath in, and exhale once again, and let a peaceful wave of relaxing energy wash over your body and mind, relaxing you completely. Pay attention to your breathing, and as you do, just allow yourself to relax even more deeply. And as you pay attention to your breathing, I'm going to count from 10 to 1, and you can just allow yourself to relax even more. And as I count, if thoughts come, just let them come and then let them go—as if they're birds or clouds just floating across the sky. . . . 10 . . . 9 . . . 8 . . . 7 . . . 6 . . . 5 . . . 4 . . . 3 . . . 2 . . . 1 . .

And when you relax this deeply, you're able to get in touch with the powerful force of healing light. You are made of light, and that light is divine. The light heals, comforts, illuminates, and transforms. There is light both within you and outside, and you can shine it on anything in your life that needs more light. The light transforms.

Just imagine now that you're able to make contact with light in one of its forms. You may see it or feel it or think about it or just know it's there. It's also okay to just make it up, imagine it, for this imagining comes from the deep inner world. In your mind's eye, you might see a pinpoint of light . . . or you may imagine an actual beam of light.

You can allow this light to beam upon you. . . . Now you may want to imagine that the light is beaming from you—from your heart, solar plexus, or the center of your forehead. . . . You may imagine yourself surrounded in light, bathed in illuminating light rays. The light can be strong or gentle. It can melt away any difficulties of your body or mind. It has profound healing power.

The light can heal any part of you inside that needs to be healed. If you like, you can allow yourself to imagine the small child inside you. The child is there inside at any age that your awareness would like for you to experience right now. Just take a moment, and allow yourself to experience that child inside you bathed in a blanket of light, healed and whole. The little child inside you is cleansed and healed with beams of light.

Now, if you have any type of ailment in your body or mind, you can just allow it to be bathed in light. . . . If you have any discomforts, they can be infused with light rays. . . .

You can also send the light to another. . . . You can bathe the entire world in illuminating beams. . . . If you like, you can send light to someone who has passed to the other side. . . .

You may experience the light as gold or white—or any other color you like. Again, it may come from a beam that originates in the universe, or it may originate from within you. It may be warm, or it may have no temperature at all. See it, feel it, know it, and let the light shine. Let it move any illusions of darkness into the reality of light.

The light within you is an embodiment of the healing power itself. Let it shine, and know the luminous presence, the great light of the universe, which transforms all darkness.

Concentrate your thought on light, rest in light, melt into light, soak yourself in light, and imagine the entire universe bathed in that light. As you do this, you may find that all the elements of your being come together as one.

You may want to contact a Great Being who exists in realms of light. If you'd like to contact one, you may allow or imagine one or more of them to illuminate your life. It can be Jesus, Moses, Buddha, Quan Yin, Mary, Saint Germain, or any other of the advanced, illumined beings. They are embodiments of the light, which permeates the entire universe. Just allow them now to bring upliftment and healing to you.

Just let yourself be uplifted, healed, and transformed in this great power of light, this sacred energy of the universe. Know that you can call to the light at any time for healing and transformation, and it will come to you. Now see if there's a word or phrase that you can use to help to bring forth the light. (pause.) You can say that word or phrase to yourself. Whenever you put your thumb together with your index finger and say your word or phrase, you're beckoning the divine energy of the light, and you find that your life is lifted to another level of being.

And so, you can get ready to come back to ordinary consciousness now. You can get ready to bring your illumination into the world. You can bring your expanded qualities back to the outer experience. If you're ready to come back now, you can allow yourself to feel very strong, alert, peaceful, and free. Feeling rested and energized, with a sense of well-being, joy, aliveness, and peace. Coming on back now . . . 1 . . . 2 . . . 3 . . . 4 . . . and 5.

MEDITATION ON
Finding and Channeling Your Wise Mind

Just get nice and comfortable now, and let yourself relax completely. Take a deep breath in, and exhale, and as you do, just let go and relax. Let your mind relax and all your thoughts, and let your body relax and all your muscles, nerves, and bones. Take another deep breath in, and exhale once again, and let a peaceful wave of relaxing energy wash over your body and mind, relaxing you completely. Pay attention to your breathing, and as you do, just allow yourself to relax even more deeply. And as you pay attention to your breathing, I'm going to count from 10 to 1, and you can just allow yourself to relax even more. And as I count, if thoughts come, just let them come and then let them go—as if they're birds or clouds just floating across the sky. . . . 10 . . . 9 . . . 8 . . . 7 . . . 6 . . . 5 . . . 4 . . . 3 . . . 2 . . . 1 . . . And as you relax this deeply, you allow yourself to get in touch with the eternal wisdom of your soul. This is your Wise Mind, a part of you that has always existed and is always ready for you at any moment, whenever you ask. Today, you'll be able to receive any communications or messages that are here for you. All you need to do is ask.

So once again, if you would, pay attention to your breathing, and see if it can become very slow and quiet. Just watch it until it does. Your breath is moving in and moving out, and as you pay attention to it, it begins to get nice and calm and slow. And now, as your breath becomes more and more peaceful, just put your attention on your eyes for a moment, and as you do, look up with your eyes still closed. Slowly bring your gaze down, and allow yourself to relax even more as your eyes come down. Do this once again, and let your eyes look up without opening them. Then let your eyes look down again. When your eyes come down, you many find yourself diving even more deeply into a state of relaxation and peace.

Now see if there's a particular topic you'd like your Wise Mind to address, a question about your life or about the life of another, or even about the world. Your question may be clear and specific. It might be about something you're experiencing right now or about something that you need to know about in your life. You may receive revelations as your Wise Mind speaks to and through you.

You may have a topic for your Wise Mind to address— or you may just want to listen to whatever it may want to share with you. Now you can allow your Wise Mind to speak to you. You listen, and you may hear a voice speaking to you or through you. It may come from one side of you or the other, or it may come from the top of your head. It may come from your heart. Notice the voice and where it comes from. Take a few moments, and listen to it. (long pause.) If you'd like to remember it, just tell yourself that you'd like to recall as many details as possible when you come back from your relaxation.

Now see if there's anything else that your Wise Mind would like to say to you. Just listen for as long as you need to. (pause.)

If you'd like to take a journey to find an embodiment of your Wise Mind, a guide, you can begin to take a journey now. You can imagine yourself walking through a wooded area or in a magnificent garden or on a sandy beach. You may see or feel it or just know it's there. You may even make it up, for this is part of your inner consciousness as well. Allow yourself to walk very slowly, noticing whatever is in your path. Soon, as you walk, you may come upon a cave. Just notice it for a moment, and see if you feel a prompting from within you to go inside. Through your curiosity, you peer into the opening of the cave, and you spot a being inside who is friendly and inviting. He or she invites you to come in (or comes to the opening of the cave) and tells you that he or she is a special emissary of the Wise Mind who wishes to give you some wisdom and understanding to bring light to your life. You notice any details about this special being, and you greet him or her or it with great love.

It may be someone new to you. Or it may be a great being you're familiar with and who is significant for your life. It may be the Universe itself that is speaking wisdom to you. You listen and find out what your Wise Mind would like for you hear. As you listen, you may want to tell yourself that you'll recall anything about this that you like. So go ahead and listen now. Feel free, if you like, to make up anything you need to. See what happens to you as you make this great connection.

(pause.)

As you simply allow your Wise Mind to speak, you find yourself moving out of the way so that you can listen to it. In truth, it's speaking all the time, and you can become relaxed enough to listen. You can contact the Wise Mind at any time, and you find yourself uplifted each time you do.

And so, you can get ready to come back to ordinary consciousness now. You can get ready to bring your wisdom and illumination into the world. You can bring your expanded qualities back to the outer experience. If you're ready to come back now, you can allow yourself to feel very strong, alert, peaceful, wise, and free. Feeling rested and energized, with a sense of well-being, joy, aliveness, and peace. Coming on back now . . . 1 . . . 2 . . . 3 . . . 4 . . . and 5.

© Marilyn Gordon, 2007

MEDITATION ON
the Wise Mind Process

Just get nice and comfortable now, and let yourself relax completely. Take a deep breath in, and exhale, and as you do, just let go and relax. Let your mind relax and all your thoughts, and let your body relax and all your muscles, nerves, and bones. Take another deep breath in, and exhale once again, and let a peaceful wave of relaxing energy wash over your body and mind, relaxing you completely. Pay attention to your breathing, and as you do, just allow yourself to relax even more deeply. And as you pay attention to your breathing, I'm going to count from 10 to 1, and you can just allow yourself to relax even more. And as I count, if thoughts come, just let them come and then let them go—as if they're birds or clouds just floating across the sky.... 10 ... 9 ... 8 ... 7 ... 6 .. . 5 ... 4 ... 3 ... 2 ... 1 ..

And as you relax this deeply, you go within yourself to a place of deep wisdom, and you know that within you is a key to resolve the challenges of your life. You can go to the very core of healing as you relax more deeply and allow yourself to experience, release, and transform whatever is in the way of relaxation and peace.

So, if you would, just take a deep look inside and see if there is a particular challenge in your life you'd like to transform. It may be in your personal life or in your work. It may be about yourself or in relationship with others. It might be an emotion, a feeling, or a pattern that has persisted. Or it might be an old experience that has been hanging around in your consciousness for too long. Just let yourself focus now on something in your life that has been difficult and that you'd like to shed light upon. (pause.)

Now allow yourself to pay attention to what is going on inside about your situation. Allow yourself to experience it in as much detail as you can. You might see it or feel it or just know it's there. If you like, you can describe your experience to yourself. It might be an experience in your body or a feeling in your heart or a thought in your mind. See what's happening with your breathing. Be with it, describe it, pay attention to it. (pause.)

Now, if you would, just take a long, slow breath in, and you imagine that you're breathing that breath directly into your experience of your issue. Breathe into your experience of it. As you breathe out, disperse it. Break it up into tiny molecules, and release it into the universe. As you exhale, you allow the solidity of your issue to change, and you breathe your issue out into the universe, breaking it up into tiny molecules, dispersing it, so it doesn't feel the same within you any longer. You can do this as many times as you like. Your breathing actually moves matter and thought or awareness, and you may be feeling very relieved. Your breathing can dissolve your issue. And as you break it up into tiny molecules, you're changing the structure of the issue. You've broken it up and released it into the universe. (pause.)

So just relax even more deeply now, and allow yourself to feel a great sense of peace. 5 . . . 4 . . . 3 . . . 2 . . . and 1.

Now you're ready to ask your Wise Mind what it would like to tell you about this. Your Wise Mind is a part of the infinite wisdom of the Universe, and it's always ready to help you to experience the expanded way of understanding your life. Now see what your Wise Mind would like to tell you about your situation. It may come as words or pictures or feelings. Just allow yourself to come to know its Infinite Power. (pause.)

Now imagine yourself as you'd like to be. You may see it or feel it, think about it, or just know it's there. It may be an experience of your unlimited expanded self—or it may be something very specific that you'd like to know or have or be or do in your life. Just let it come forth in any way your consciousness would like for you to experience it. You are creating a new vision for yourself, your life, and the world. You realize what's possible for you in your highest potential. (pause.) Next you can find a word or phrase that symbolizes this transformation, and if you like you can put your thumb and index finger together and say this word or phrase to yourself as many times as you like. (pause.) You are saving your transformation inside your being, and it has great power for you when you say it any time of the day or night.

So now, just allow yourself to experience the results of your Wise Mind Process for transformation and healing. If there is more to heal, you can always do that. You can do the process as many times as you like with your eyes either open or closed. As you do the process, you feel more and more energized and happy and free. You are releasing obstacles that may have been in the way of experiencing your radiant and powerful being.

And so, you can get ready to come back to ordinary consciousness now. You can get ready to bring your healing and wisdom into the world. You can bring your expanded qualities back to the outer experience. If you're ready to come back now, you can allow yourself to feel very strong, alert, peaceful, and very free. Feeling rested and energized, with a sense of well-being, joy, aliveness, and peace. Coming on back now . . . 1 . . . 2 . . . 3 . . . 4 . . . and 5.

©Marilyn Gordon 2007

MEDITATION ON
the Heart of Compassion

Just get nice and comfortable now, and let yourself relax completely. Take a deep breath in, and exhale, and as you do, just let go and relax. Let your mind relax and all your thoughts, and let your body relax and all your muscles, nerves, and bones. Take another deep breath in, and exhale once again, and let a peaceful wave of relaxing energy wash over your body and mind, relaxing you completely. Pay attention to your breathing, and as you do, just allow yourself to relax even more deeply. And as you pay attention to your breathing, I'm going to count from 10 to 1, and you can just allow yourself to relax even more. And as I count, if thoughts come, just let them come and then let them go—as if they're birds or clouds just floating across the sky . . . 10 . . . 9 . . . 8 . . . 7 . . . 6 . . . 5 . . . 4 . . . 3 . . . 2 . . . 1 . .

And as you relax this deeply, you go within yourself to a soft, comfortable place in which you may be able to feel your heart opening more and more. And as you enter this deep, soft place within yourself, you begin to step back and look at your life and the lives of others. From this vantage point, you can understand that everyone is acting out a particular life path on the stage of eternity like actors with scripts, and that most people know not what they do. Many have a lack of awareness of the spiritual truths to one extent or another, and most people experience many difficulties. You can then let your awareness lead you to a state of deep compassion, a special kind of love that includes understanding.

First you may want to start with experiencing compassion for yourself. You may have had very difficult experiences in life or excess baggage that you're carrying. As you step back and see this, you can have compassion for all you're doing, considering all the challenges. You can also have compassion for all the parts of your own self that you're healing. This compassion has the power to heal. So, if you would, just let yourself feel the kindness and loving compassion for yourself and your great ability to survive and to move forward. You may feel the compassion as a hand that touches you gently, in the same way that Mother Teresa might put her hand on yours and send you blessings. Perhaps you can feel this compassion in your heart, and you can allow everything in you to soften and become warmed with this beautiful compassionate healing power. You might have an image of yourself filled with compassion or of being compassionately cared for, or you might just think about it or know it's there. (pause.)

Next you can have compassion for a part of yourself that has been waiting for so long for this tender loving care. It may be you as a child or a teen or an adult—a part of you that has been waiting to be awakened by your compassionate care. Just allow this part of you to experience the power of this compassion, and see if there's a transformation that takes place as you lovingly become the channel for this healing power to occur. (pause.)

You can begin to open up to the true reality that you are ultimately loved and cared for, and you may want to come back to the truth of who you are—a radiant being of infinite light, love, and compassion. You may want to understand that the difficulties that you've experienced in your consciousness have led you to seek a higher life, and so they've pierced you open to understand and experience the truths of the Universe more fully. Truly, everyone and everything is the universal life force in disguise.

So as you relax even more deeply, you can also float and drift into a profound state of awareness in which you understand the spiritual truth here that "others" are really parts of your own self. In the highest truth, we're all One. We are all a part of one another, and the compassion you have for anyone who seems to be "another" is the same compassion that you can have for yourself.

So just let yourself feel this compassion in your heart of hearts. Feel its softness and kindness and mercy. Just allow yourself to allow the old boundaries to dissolve, as you merge with the All That Is, and you connect with all of life. It's good for you to allow this kindness into your heart and into your life. Whenever you do, great healing takes place in everything you are and everything you do.

And so, you can get ready to come back to ordinary consciousness now. You can get ready to bring your healing and compassion into the world. You can bring your expanded qualities back to the outer experience. If you're ready to come back now, you can allow yourself to feel very strong, alert, peaceful, and very free. Feeling rested and energized, with a sense of well-being, joy, aliveness, and peace. Coming on back now . . . 1 . . . 2 . . . 3 . . . 4 . . . and 5.

© *Marilyn Gordon, 2007*

MEDITATION ON
Deep Peace

Just get nice and comfortable now, and let yourself relax completely. Take a deep breath in, and exhale, and as you do, just let go and relax. Let your mind relax and all your thoughts, and let your body relax and all your muscles, nerves, and bones. Take another deep breath in, and exhale once again, and let a peaceful wave of relaxing energy wash over your body and mind, relaxing you completely. Pay attention to your breathing, and as you do, just allow yourself to relax even more deeply. And as you pay attention to your breathing, I'm going to count from 10 to 1, and you can just allow yourself to relax even more. And as I count, if thoughts come, just let them come and then let them go—as if they're birds or clouds just floating across the sky . . . 10 . . . 9 . . . 8 . . . 7 . . . 6 . . . 5 . . . 4 . . . 3 . . . 2 . . . 1 . .

And as you relax this deeply, you allow yourself to go to an even more profound level of yourself where there is pure peace. You can listen to the words of the great poet Rumi, who said,

> Out beyond ideas of wrongdoing and rightdoing, there is a field. I'll meet you there.

> When the Soul lies down in that grass,
> The world is too full to talk about.

So you lie down in that grass, and you allow yourself to experience your breathing at an even deeper level. Your breath moves in and your breath moves out, and you understand that this is the flow of the universe. Your breath is the energy of the universe, and you are the energy of the universe. You understand this as you take the time now to dive into the center of yourself, where there is pure peace. You can go to the core of the Self, the still point of the inner world, the place that is the beginning and end of all healing and transformation.

This experience of peace may be without words or pictures or sounds. Or it may bring forth images or words or sounds that evoke this deep experience in you. You may have these experiences of peace. Or you may know the experience of total stillness and quiet that lives at the center of your true nature.

This is a sanctuary in your soul. When you come to this central core of peace within yourself, you can understand everything in your life from another perspective. Here in this core, you listen or feel or watch, and healing comes through. You're given the opportunity to be more peaceful about any of the issues of your life or in the world, and you can know that everything that's taking place is but a type of illusion, and your soul, the peace, and your higher being are the ultimate truths of existence.

Here is a place in which you can shift your perspective, reminding you that ultimately everything is peace at its deepest core—even illusions that seem so unlike it. Yet as you dive down into it, there is nothing but infinite peace. Here you can rest beside the still waters, here the wars have ended, and here you can find the healing for your soul. Stillness itself can even be the answer you're looking for. When you're still, you stop your thoughts, and you understand that just by being quiet, you've taken a leap into another level of your consciousness. "Peace, be still and know that I AM God." Stillness itself is the answer.

If you asked your Wise Mind, it might say this to you:

> Peace is the greatest gift in the universe, as it is pure gold itself. "I AM the peace of God" is what you are inside. I AM showing you the way out of your dilemmas. Just be still for a moment. You are caught up in the letters of the alphabet, your thoughts. Just be quiet for a moment, and give yourself the opportunity to attune to the stillness deep inside yourself. You're not who you think you are. You're boundless and eternal. This peace is a state of great healing, and it's giving you great gifts. Come in peace and silence to the truths of the Universe, and you will find the way to the heart and soul of all things.

Peace, wisdom, love, light, compassion, forgiveness—all of these carry you across the great ocean of consciousness. All of these qualities are woven from the same fabric as the Wise Mind, and all are qualities of the Infinite. The experience of deep peace transforms everything in your life.

And so, you can get ready to come back to regular waking consciousness now. You can get ready to bring your deep stillness and peace into the world. You can bring your expanded qualities back to the outer experience. If you're ready to come back now, you can allow yourself to feel very strong, alert, peaceful, and free. Feeling rested and energized, with a sense of well-being, joy, aliveness, and deep peace. Coming on back now . . . 1 . . . 2 . . . 3 . . . 4 . . . and 5.

© Marilyn Gordon, 2007

Notes

i   Coleman Barks, ed. and trans., The Essential Rumi (New York: Castle Books, 1995) p. 101

ii   Thich Nhat Hanh, Peace Is Every Step (New York: Bantam, 1991) p.82

iii   Quoted by Larry Rosenberg, "From Mindfulness to Awareness," Shambhala Sun, July 2003.

iv   Percy B. Shelley, "Adonais: An Elegy on the Death of John Keats," available at http://www.theotherpages.org/poems/shell03.html (July 1, 2007).

v   Marilyn Gordon, Extraordinary Healing (Oakland: Wise Word Publishing, 2000), available for purchase at http://www.hypnotherapycenter.com.

vi   Grady Claire Porter, The Journey (Tucson, Celebration Publishing, 2002).p.93

vii   Omraam Mikhaël Aïvanhov, Light Is a Living Spirit (Editions Prosveta, France) p.58

viii Coleman Barks and Michael Green, A Journal with the Poetry of Rumi (Sausalito, Brush Dance, 1999).

ix A Course in Miracles (New York: Foundation for Inner Peace, 1975), vol. 2, lesson 50.

x Guy Warren Ballard, The "I AM" Discourses, by the Ascended Master, Saint Germain (Chicago: Saint Germain Press, 1940) p. 39.

xi Walt Whitman, "Song of Myself," Leaves of Grass, http://www.princeton.edu/~batke/logr/log_026.html (July 1, 2007).

xii Shahriar Shahriari, "Rumi 116," http://www.rumionfire.com/shams/rumi116.htm (July 10, 2007).

xiii Thich Nhat Hanh, "Please Call Me by My True Names," from Peace Is Every Step: The Path of Mindfulness in Everyday Life (New York: Bantam, 1991), p. 123.

For information on Marilyn Gordon's talks, workshops, intensives, certification programs, books, manuals, CDs, DVDs and more, see:

www.hypnotherapycenter.com
and
www.thewisemind.com

To book Marilyn Gordon for speaking events and to find out more about the Wise Mind Transformation Seminars, contact:

WiseWord Publishing
PO Box 10795
Oakland CA 94606
Telephone: (510) 839-4800
or 1(800) 398-0034
Fax: (510) 836-0477

Email: mgordon@hypnotherapycenter.com

Also available from

WiseWord Publishing and Marilyn Gordon

CDs and DVDs
The Wise Mind spoken word CDs
Individually-produced CDs for your needs
Workshop CDs
The Transformational Healing Method (THM) DVD

Books and Manuals
Extraordinary Healing
Healing is Remembering Who You Are
And various transformational manuals

Certification Programs and Workshops
Regularly scheduled workshops and intensives
offering you the opportunity to become a
Certified Hypnotherapist. A first-rate training program
that gives you skills for doing high quality work,
a "school for your soul."
Special workshops & Wise Mind Transformation seminars,
Teleseminars and Telecourses

Web Sites and Email
www.hypnotherapycenter.com
www.thewisemind.com
www.lifetransformationsecrets.com
mgordon@hypnotherapycenter.com

About the Author

Marilyn Gordon is a board certified hypnotherapist, teacher, speaker, healer, school director and author with over thirty years of experience and a diverse and expansive background in teaching and healing. She is the award-winning founder and director of the Center for Hypnotherapy Certification in Oakland, California, has been recognized in 14 *Who's Whos*, appears on radio and television, and gives numerous workshops. She is also the author of *Extraordinary Healing: Transforming Your Consciousness, Your Energy System and Your Life*, as well as other books, manuals, CDs and DVDs. She works in the area of profound mental-emotional-spiritual transformation. She does her best to bring compassion, inspiration, and love to all she does. Her purpose is to work with love and wisdom to amplify the good and talents in others and to assist them in transforming their consciousness and empowering their lives.